THE
ORIGIN OF THE MOVING SCHOOL IN MASSACHUSETTS

BY

HARLAN UPDEGRAFF, Ph.D.

Chief of Alaska Division, U. S. Bureau of Education, and
sometime Assistant in Philosophy and Education, Columbia
University, and Fellow in Education, Teachers College.

TEACHERS COLLEGE, COLUMBIA UNIVERSITY
CONTRIBUTIONS TO EDUCATION, NO. 17

D1202271

PUBLIS.
𝔗eachers College, Columbia University
NEW YORK CITY
1908

Library of Congress Cataloging in Publication Data

Updegraff, Harlan, 1874-
    The origin of the moving school in Massachusetts.

    Original ed. issued as no. 17 of Teachers College,
Columbia University. Contributions to education.
    Originally presented as the author's thesis, Columbia.
    Bibliography: p.
    1. Education--Massachusetts--History. 2. School
management and organization--Massachusetts. I. Title.
II. Series: Columbia University. Teachers College.
Contributions to education, no. 17.
LA304.U7 1972   370'.9744   78-177685
ISBN 0-404-55017-7
ISBN 0-404-55000-2 (set)

Reprinted by Special Arrangement with Teachers
College Press, Columbia University, New York

From the edition of 1908: New York
First AMS edition published in 1972
Manufactured in th United States

AMS PRESS, INC.
NEW YORK, N.Y. 10003

Columbia University

Contributions to Education

Teachers College Series

No. 17

AMS PRESS

NEW YORK

PREFACE

This study aims to treat intensively the subject of school control in Massachusetts from the time of settlement to the first decades of the eighteenth century and to account for that development in so far as it bore upon the creation of the moving school. Because of the close connection between the abolition of the tuition-tax and the establishment of the moving school it is necessary to describe the evolution of school support during the same period.

The first four chapters—those which deal with the evolution of school control and of school support—may not seem to be logically connected with the subject proper. They are, in fact, an introduction to it, made necessary for the reasons that school control up to the present time has been considered as progressing during the seventeenth century from control of the many to control of the few, whereas the reverse is the truth; and also because no study has yet been made, and the results presented, of the subject of school support for this period. While there is a unity in the whole by reason of the fact that it was written from a single point of view—that of describing in a complete manner the origin of the moving school, yet the discussion of the reasons for its creation begins with Chapter V. The preceding chapters serve the purpose of paving the way for a satisfactory presentation of the subject proper as contained in the last six chapters.

Two appendices are added which contain all the official local records bearing upon schools that are extant up to 1648. The purpose in presenting this material is to aid the reader in reflecting for himself upon the conclusion of the text concerning the records of these earliest years, which are so difficult to interpret satisfactorily. It must not be forgotten, however, that when the material is so meagre the grounds for a proper point of view in their interpretation can be determined only as a result of a very careful consideration of the entire system of civil administration as it existed, and of the practices in school administration both previous and subsequent to that time.

My gratitude for help in this study is due especially to President Nicholas Murray Butler under whose instruction interest in this line of study was stimulated, to Professor Herbert L. Osgood, who has been very helpful in all questions relating to the development of civil institutions, and to Professor Paul Monroe, under whose immediate direction the work was done, and who has contributed much by kindly criticism and suggestion to all phases of the study.

Bureau of Education.

February, 1908.

CONTENTS

4 *Contents.*

Chapter VII

Intellectual Decline

Chapter VIII

Decentralizing Tendencies of Democracy

Chapter IX

The Dame School

6   *Contents.*

CHAPTER X
The Abolition of the Tuition-Tax

Conclusion

INTRODUCTION

The town in Massachusetts was the original local unit for control of schools. The school district was evolved out of the town through a long process extending from the middle of the seventeenth century to about the close of the first quarter in the nineteenth century. The moving school was the first and most distinctive step in that process. Roughly the period of its general dominance was the first half of the eighteenth century. This study is an attempt to account for the establishment of the moving school. Speaking generally, it was wanted because the central original fixed, or standing, school failed to satisfy longer the new conditions arising in the development of colonial life, Many of these new conditions were in themselves a product of slow growth, extending back over the entire latter half of the seventeenth century. As a result this treatment deals for the most part with the life of this earlier period.

This study properly belongs to the history of school administration. As such it lies both in the field of the history of education and of political history. From the standpoint of the former the creation of the moving school may be studied as throwing light upon the efficiency of the school district as an educational institution; from the point of view of political history the movement may be regarded as an evolution of a new organ of local government. This study aims to satisfy both points of view. By showing the educational situation which gave rise to the institution, a basis of criticism is established which has its application to the present problem of the abolition of the school district. On the other hand, by considering the control of schools as but one of the many subjects of local administration, some of which were closely related to it and passing through a similar process of evolution, the subject is treated as an evolution of a new political institution. As such the school district must possess great interest, for it displays the genius of the American people in the construction of a new type of institution to meet a new situation. Of all the steps in the process leading to its formation, the moving school will ever claim the greatest attention, as it was in its creation that this genius reached its highest flight. It is also true that the remarkable part in the entire process was confined to the first step. The later development was a result of familiar tendencies which are always working in the body politic and was characterized by a gradual even advance, while the moving school was a great step forward and the beginning of a different order of things.

To understand the rise of the moving school, it is necessary to understand the character of the control of the town school and its tendencies from the time of its establishment., This is to be determined primarily by a study of the town records. For the distribution of powers between the central and local governments gave large powers to the town in strictly local affairs; and in the matter of methods of school control there was little interference by the General Court. Its efforts were directed toward strengthening the work that the agencies of the local governments should do rather than toward prescribing what agencies should perform it.

While the creation of the moving school as a step in the evolution of the school district is properly a subject in the evolution of school control, yet its establishment was closely related with a distinctive change in the methods of school support. In consequence, to understand fully the rise of the moving school it is necessary to know the character and tendencies of school support subsequent to the time of its formation. This information is to be obtained from the town records for the same reasons as stated in the preceding paragraph.

The evolution of school control and the evolution of school support were closely united. They were interdependent, profoundly affecting each other. There were two distinct periods in their evolution, first that of the church-town school from the beginning to 1647, and that of the civil school from 1647 to the time of the establishment of the moving school. This division into periods will be observed in their treatment, first studying *the methods of raising the master's salary* in the church-town school and then in the civil school, and then the *distribution of the functions of control between the various governmental agencies* in each of the two periods. In this way the close relation between the movements may be shown.

After the way has thus been prepared the bearing of the social, economic, and general political development of the same periods whereby the stationary central school was rendered unsatisfactory and a new institution required in order to meet the situation, may be intelligently appreciated. This development will be presented under the headings of Social Disintegration, Dispersion of Population, Intellectual Decline, and Decentralizing Tendencies of Democracy.

But there was another influence outside of this field which had a great deal to do with the founding of the moving school. It was the existence of private master's and dame's schools. Of these, the latter is best known and was probably on the whole the more influential. They are both discussed under the heading, The Dame School. Finally, as the most immediate cause of the creation of the moving school, Abolition of the Tuition Tax is presented. In this chapter connection is made with the previous treatment of the evolution of school support. The causes of this particular step are set forth and its important bearing upon the establishment of the moving school fully demonstrated.

CHAPTER I

CONTROL AND SUPPORT OF THE CHURCH-TOWN SCHOOL

PART I METHODS OF SUPPORT

1635-1647

The school of the Puritan was a very simple institution compared with the school of today. It was held in one room, usually in a private house, and taught as a rule by a single teacher. There were both the private school taught by a master, and the school which the local government controlled in some way, and which for that reason may be called the town school. It is generally accepted to be true that the private school antedates the town school and that they existed side by side throughout all the colonial history.

The establishment of a town school as distinct from a private school was wholly a matter of local initiative until 1647. In this year a law was passed compelling all towns of fifty householders and over to have a school open to all the children in the town. With the motives that led these church-towns to provide a town school we are not here concerned. It is rather the political aspect of their action which we must notice. Legally the General Court was the source of all governmental authority and the towns could perform only acts which had the warrant of this supreme power. But from the beginning the town met in town meeting—the general court of the settlement—elected officers, legislated upon some matters of purely local concern without interference and apparently with the full, though tacit, approval of the General Court.[1] Finally the right to do so was confirmed by an express act of the colonial legislature in the year 1636. This act ratified and confirmed the course of procedure already practiced by the towns and in granting them the authortiy " to make such orders as may concern the well ordering of their towns not repugnant to the laws and orders here established by the General Court "[2] gave them a wide range of power for the future.

(1) Salem Recs. p. 7.
(2) Mass. Col. Recs. I. p. 172.

The principle of local initiative was legally established in local civil affairs by this act. The continued observance of it in educational affairs has caused local practice to be in advance of central legislation in the framing of institutions.

In the dozen years preceding the passage of the first colonial law regarding schools different towns proceeded in the establishment of a town school under this general grant of power. As it was purely a local affair each town proceeded in its own way. In consequence there resulted a great variety in the details of control and support. In these first two chapters an attempt will be made to determine the nature of the common fundamental elements in the variety of plans and processes.

When a town took action concerning a school it did so by means of the agencies of local government already established, or, if these were not satisfactory or sufficient, it created others. These were the town meeting, and its subordinate agencies, the selectmen, the permanent school committee, and the temporary committee. The last need receive but little attention in these first two chapters, however, because of its rarity and comparative unimportance:

The town meeting was an assembly of all those who were eligible to vote on town affairs. Eligibility did not rest on the narrow qualification of church membership that was fundamental in colonial citizenship. From the very beginning the " freemen " of the colonial government admitted those who were not church members into the local corporation and gave them their votes. This custom was legalized by the action of the General Court in 1635[1] and more specifically defined in 1647.[2]   Thus the action, of town meetings upon schools have always been acts of bodies which in theory at least were democratic.[3]

By the word " selectmen " we mean here to designate those bodies of men who were appointed by the town meetings to perform a certain class of functions, and known variously as the " selectmen," which became the common term later, the " selected townsmen," " ye chosen men for managing the prudential affairs," the " prudential men," " the town representative," the " five," the " seven," the " nine," or " thirteen " men.[4]   In

---

(1) Mass. Col. Recs. .I. p. 161.
(2) Ibid II. p. 197.
(3) A "valid vote" must have had the support of a majority of the "freemen" either in town meeting or in the selectmen's meeting.
(4) Howard, Local Const. Hist. p. 74; Doyle, English Colonies II.; p. 11.

general they may be regarded as the ministerial officers of the town meeting.

The school committee performed the duties and exercised the powers fixed upon it by the town meeting. The functions are usually definitely stated; so, there is little uncertainty as to its powers.

Having described the agencies of local government, let us now proceed to define the functions of government performed by them. As in all cases of distribution of governmental powers they may be divided into the legislative and administrative functions, the former embracing the expression of the will of the people of the town, and the latter the execution of that will as expressed.[1] The legislative and administrative functions included doubtless great variety of detail, but only the necessary actions—the minimum amount necessary to secure the establishment and continuance of a town school—need here be considered.

These were as follows:

1. Legislative functions.
    a. Decision to have a school—i.e., to secure a master.
    b. Election of the master.
    c. Determination of how master should be paid.
    d. The amount to be paid master, or,
    e. Length of term.

2. Administrative functions.
    Securing the money to pay the master, aiding in the finding of a master, fixing the time for his school to begin, renting of house for his school when there was no town house for the school, providing fuel, fixing school hours, making incidental rules and regulations, paying the master, etc.

In regard to this outline of minimum governmental action several things should be said. In the first place, it cannot be applied to any one town on account of the variety of methods used in the various towns. Second, the entire scheme emphasizes the master, for the reason that he was the primary and almost the sole factor in many of the schools except the scholars, and the only one dealt with in the town records with that degree of frequency and continuity which enables the student to analyze

---

[1] Goodnow, Politics and Administration pp. 16-23.

and trace the development of control and support. Third, the election of the master is placed under the head of legislative action, because it was regarded as one of the functions of government which should be participated in by all the people in the primary assembly. He was looked upon in much the same way as the pastor of the church.[1] Fourth, the scheme presents an arbitrary division: the validity or invalidity of this division is of no importance, however, in the conclusions.

This study of school control and support must determine which of the agencies performed these various functions during this period of the church-town school; and also what methods were used in supporting the master. As dealing with matters of support constituted some of the prominent governmental functions concerning the school, it follows that the decision as to the agency adopted to carry on the legislative and administrative features connected with support would be conditioned by the methods of raising the money. It will therefore facilitate the progress of this study and secure a clearer understanding of the situation to examine the records first with the point in view of determining the manner in which the towns secured the money to support the master of these town schools.

The meagreness, indefiniteness, and the small number of the records bearing upon schools present many obstacles to the student. It is possible to fill in the skeleton of knowledge they furnish of school control and support for different conceptions of what was done. In consequence this study has required extreme caution. It was necessary to apply constantly certain principles of historical interpretation. These the reader must likewise bear in mind. They presented themselves to the author as he began his study, as follows:

First, as institutions do not spring up full-fledged from the mind of man, but rather are the gradual outgrowth of those which preceded them, so it is to be expected that the agencies of control and methods of support of the Puritan school were shaped to some extent at least by, if not literally copied after, the practices of school administration as they existed previously and contemporaneously in England. It is, therefore, necessary that these English practices be kept constantly in mind in the interpretation of the records.

---

[1] De Montmorency, State intervention in English Education, pp. 101-2.

Second, though previous institutions furnish the basis upon which new institutions are founded, the entire life of the people who modify the old in the construction of the new plays a prominent part in the process. It is, therefore, necessary that one understand the relation of the school to the other institutions in the colonial society, the political theories of the Puritans particularly as they bore upon local government, and their practices in the support and control of other public enterprises. All these features of the new elements in the Puritan civilization must be given due weight in reaching our conclusions.

Third, the interpretation given to the records must be consistent with an orderly evolution of institutions from this period to the following. It is requisite also that this evolution be satisfactorily accounted for.

Fourth, when the above standards fail to point to one conclusion, it may then be taken into account that the Puritans were an eminently practical people. It was their habit to take the " short cut " and to choose the method which seemed the simplest and most direct.

Fifth, all preconceptions of Puritan practices must be laid aside, and the reading into the past of present conditions avoided.

Methods of Raising the Master's Salary [1]

The sources of school support in general use during the early seventeenth century in England were annuities from the crown, rent from land, income from endowment, and tuition. No instance of the levying of a civil tax is known to have occurred; and certainly it was not a common thing for a town to take money out of its treasury for the support of any school within its limits.[2] It can be safely said that the levying of a local tax, if it ever did occur, was so singular and rare a thing that it could not have produced any appreciable influence upon the Massachusetts settlers.

To the Puritan in Europe and in England the school was subordinate to the church; its chief object was to secure the establishment of the " true religion," [3] or as it is stated in another

---

[1] The references to the town records before 1647 are not given in the text but in the appendix in connection with the records as there given. The reader should consult the appendix frequently.

[2] Monroe. Hist. of Education, 393-5; Stow. The Elizabethan Grammar-Schools. *In preparation.*

[3] Ibid, pp. 433-7. Grant's *Burgh Schools of Scotland*, pp. 76-80.

place, " the education of children in piety, and good literature."
This subordination of school to church is shown most clearly
among the English Puritans in the Welsh Education Act, passed
by the Cromwellian parliament in 1649. Its title " an Act for
the better Propagation and Preaching of the Gospel in Wales
and Redress of Some Grievances " reveals its tenor. It provided
for the appointment of Commissioners who among other things,
had the right to grant certificates to " Ministers of the Gospel
...... for the preaching of the Gospel...... in settled Congregations and Parochial charges...... or for the keeping of
Schools and Education of Children."[1]

Their views as to methods of support of schools were under
such conditions, strengthened by the force of practice of the
preceding centuries, inseparably bound up with the methods of
the support of the church. This is shown in this same act. The
commissioners were directed to receive and disperse " all and
singular the rents, issues, and profits of all ecclesiastical livings
within the disposal of parliament provided that the yearly maintenance of a Minister do not exceed one hundred pounds, and the
yearly maintenance of a School-master exceed not forty
pounds."[2] The most prominent school founded under the provisions of this act was supported by endowment. Another instance of this close connection of church and school is seen in
Chapter 31 of the year 1649. By it the first-fruits and tenths
created by Henry VIII were vested in trustees upon trust " to
pay yearly all such salaries, stipends, allowances, and provisions,
as have been limited or appointed for preaching the Gospel,
Preaching Ministers, or Schoolmasters or others in England or
Wales, settled or confirmed by Ordinance or Order of Parliament." In the event, however, that the amount of first-fruits
and tenths did not reach £20,000, then " some other part of the
yearly revenue payable into the exchequer should be provided to
make up the deficiency." [3]

---

[1] De Montmorency, State Intervention, p. 102.
[2] Ibid, p. 102.
[3] Ibid. pp. 103-4. NOTE.—Although there is nothing to show positively that the
measures framed in the efforts of the Puritan to establish schools in other countries had
a direct influence upon the plans of the Massachusetts settlers, yet even if there was
a bond of connection between the movements, there is nothing in the history of education in these countries that materially differs from the situation in England as set forth
in these two acts. Monroe, Hist. of Education, pp. 433-7. Grant, pp. 76-80

The Puritan in America undoubtedly adhered to the same fundamental views regarding the relation of the school to the church and the sources of its support as did the Puritan in England. While some features of the English laws of 1649 are the effect of the experiences of Massachusetts in dealing with the questions of schools, yet the fundamental proposition in the Welsh Education Act regarding support, that the school should be supported from the church funds, had undoubtedly been held by all the Puritans for over a half century before the emigration to America. It may therefore be affirmed that it is reasonable to expect that this principle was carried out in America.

This necessitates an inquiry into the sources of support of the church in Massachusetts. It is to be expected at the outset that it will be different from that referred to in the acts of 1649 because of the difference in conditions. Inquiry shows that the first method was the contribution, the second, its lineal descendant, the compulsory contribution.

The "contribution" as it was first spoken of was grounded upon the practice of the early church at Corinth. Authority was given for its use in December 1633 when "after much deliberation and serious advice, the Lord directed the teacher Mr. Cotton, to make it clear by Scriptures, that the minister's maintenance, as well as all other charges of the church, should be defrayed out of a stock or treasury, which was to be raised out of the weekly contribution, which accordingly was agreed upon." [1] It became a regular feature of the Sunday service, and is thus described by Lechford, " Prior to the dispersion of the people in the afternoon, a contribution is taken. One of the deacons, saying, ' Brethren of the congregation, as God has prospered you, so freely offer,' the magistrates and chief gentlemen first, and then the elders and all the congregation of men, and most of them that are not of the church, all single persons, widows and women, in absence of their husbands, come up one after another one way, and bring their offerings to the deacon at his seat, and put it into a box of wood for the purpose if it be money or paper; if it be any other chattel, they set or lay it down before the deacons, and so pass another way to their seats again." [2]

[1] Felt, Ecclesiastical History of N, E. I. p. 162.
[2] Ibid. I. p. 433.

The example set by the Boston church was generally followed.[1] It was the substitute for the tithe of the old church, which in many respects it resembles. Like it, the " stock " thus raised was spent for the maintenance of the clergy, the preservation of the fabric or church buildings, and the benefit of the poor.[2] Of these three avenues of expenditure the first persisted in America the longest. Some of the congregations at first built their meeting houses from the proceeds of the rate, as at Watertown.[3] However as late as 1641 at least, the contribution was still generally used for this second purpose. Lechford tells us that on " extraordinary occasions, as the building or repairing of the meeting house and other necessities, the ministers press a liberal contribution with effectual exhortation out of the Scriptures."[4] Watertown in 1642 levied a " rate " for the support of the poor and Salem in 1643 began aiding the poor by a tax levied upon the inhabitants.[5] On the other hand in Boston as late as 1684 the original custom continued.[6] The practice of supporting the minister continued in Boston for over a century, [7] but by 1660, it had been given up in practically all other towns.[8]

It was abandoned because it was not successful. Of this feature Prince quaintly says speaking of Plymouth, " But growing in knowledge and I suppose in the apprehension that such a practice was peculiarly accommodated to the age of inspiration (1 Cor. XIV, 30) which they never pretended to, they, after gradually lay it down." [9] In Massachusetts the difficulty did not lie wholly with the church members, the more covetous of whom were inclined to give too little and the liberal too much. Those who were not members of the church were naturally opposed to aiding in the support of it. Oftentimes the church found its " stock " depleted, and at the same time, its officers had certain knowledge of the lack of adequate contribution by some of the members or inhabitants of the town.[10] It was necessary for the support of the church that more rigorous

---

(1) Felt, Eccle. Hist. I. p. 174.
(2) Gneist, History of the English Constitution, II. p. 205. Note 2a.
(3) Watertown Recs,. I. p. 1.
(4) Ibid, I. p. 9.
(5) Salem Recs., p. 120.
(6) Dexter, Congregationalism as seen in its Literature, p. 454.
(7) Palfry, Hist. of N. E II. p. 38.
(8) A report to the legislature in 1657, gives only three towns (Hingham, Weymouth and Braintree, as preserving the custom, Felt, Eccle. Hist. II. p. 160.
(9) Quoted by Felt, Eccle. Hist. I. p. 162.
(10) Ibid, II p. 174.

measures be taken. The state was called upon to enforce the demands of the church. The compulsory contribution resulted.

The first use of this term we have found is in an act of the General Court in 1638, which reads,— "This court taking into consideration the necessity of an equal contribution to all common charges in towns, and observing that the chief occasion of the defect herein ariseth from hence, that many of those who are not freemen, nor members of any church, do take advantage to withdraw their help in such voluntary contributions as are in use.

"It is therefore hereby declared, that every inhabitant in any town is liable to contribute to all charges, both in church and commonwealth whereof he doth, or may receive benefit: and withal it is also ordered, that every such inhabitant who shall not contribute, proportionately to his ability with other freemen of the same town, to all common charges, as well for upholding the ordinance in the churches as otherwise shall be compelled thereto by assessment and distress to be levied by the constable, or other officers of the towns, or in other cases."[1]

Many of the church-towns took advantage of the law at once, but in different ways. A typical case is that of Salem. The records of the town meeting in the following year state that "there was a voluntary town contribution toward the maintenance of the ministry, quarterly to be paid.

"The vote thereof remaineth with the Deacons."[2]

Boston pursued a similar plan for some years in accordance with Cotton's advice in favor of "a voluntary contribution" to be collected quarterly.[3] Watertown is typical of another class. By 1642 it had resorted to taxation.[4] Salem in 1645 ordered that the non-members of the congregation shall be rated.[5] The difficulty met in securing the pastor's maintenance was doubtless increased by the stringent economic conditions which prevailed during the first few years of the fifth decade.

The law of 1638 applied also, doubtless, to the collection for the poor, and for the building of churches. The abandonment

---

(1) Mass. Col. Recs. I. pp. 240-1.
(2) Salem Recs. p. 93.
(3) Felt, Eccle. Hist. I. p. 389.
(4) Watertown Recs. I. p. 9.
(5) Note the language—*congregation* used as equivalent to *town*. The church members evidently were not "rated." Salem Recs. p. 140.

of it for these purposes earlier than for the ministry and the adoption of the regular town rate was caused probably to some extent by the influence of the examples of the " church rate " and the " poor rate " in the English parish. There is an interesting parallel between the development of the " church rate " and the " poor rate " in the English parish and the town rate in Massachusetts for building and repairing the church and for the aid of the poor.[1] All went through the stages of free contribution, compulsory contribution, and civil tax.

The possibility of connection between these movements in America and England is strengthened by the fact that the entire evolution of the poor rate in England was worked out during the reign of Elizabeth, which places the latter part of the movement within the lives of some of the colonists.

We are now prepared to place ourselves in the same situation in which the Puritans found themselves in deciding the question of the support of the master. Those in the first emigration had an intimate acquaintance undoubtedly with the chartered schools and the methods of their support. On the other hand they had not come in direct contact with any distinctly Puritan school. The distinctly Puritan element was with him theoretical, while the English element was real and actual in his experience.

The first schools were private schools, like those kept by a master in England, without a foundation of any sort. The master got his return in form of tuition. Upon these schools the people looked kindly, and oftentimes through the town corporations gave them substantial aid styled usually " an encouragement." The General Court at times took notice of the good work done by a Latin master and rewarded him. Newbury in 1639 gave Anthony Somerby a few acres of upland and salt marsh, Cambridge on several occasions gave Elijah Cortlett money, and the General Court presented him a piece of land.[2] But these private schools had two notable deficiencies from the Puritan point of view. They were not permanent; they did not offer opportunity for the education of those children whose parents were either unable to educate them and to pay the tuition

---

[1] Gneist, II. pp. 195-207.   Nichols, Hist. of the Eng. Poor Law. II. pp. 149-193. Howard, p. 33.
[2] Currier, Newbury, p. 395.   Cambridge Recs., p. 97.   Paige, Cambridge, p. 367. Mass. Col. Recs., IV. pp. 16, 284, 486.

fees. Schools, in their opinion, should be provided, which would satisfy this requirement in order to secure the perpetuity of the social and political order they had established.

In answer to this demand the town schools were established. But in these days of early beginnings in the new home, when institutions were undergoing a process of transition, fine distinctions were not made between the character of acts. The people wanted a school; they took the most direct and convenient way to secure one. Sometimes this was done in a town meeting, sometimes not, as in Boston in 1636; one town (Roxbury) even went so far in its desire to secure permanency as to draw up a charter and have it confirmed by the General Court. But they were all town schools, except Roxbury, because they were open to all the children of the town whether their parents contributed to the support of the master or not.

Let us now examine their recorded acts in the endeavor to determine as fully and as accurately as we may what were the sources from which they drew the support of the master.

The fact that the town corporation owned much undivided land caused the adoption of the method of support from land. In this way the congregation gave as a whole, rather than individually, and no one had to give up anything which had previously been a source of revenue to him. Many towns adopted this method. Boston in 1642 set apart Deare Island,[1] Dorchester in 1639, Thomson's Island,[2] Dedham in 1645, 40 to 60 acres of public land which had previously been set apart for public use.[3] The two former towns got some income, though the inhabitants of Dorchester must have been considerably disappointed in the amount.[4] Charleston in 1647 got some income from both the rent of an island and a weir.[5] The reasons for the failure of this source of support to bring anything more than a small percentage of the total outlay, was the plentifulness of land. Land was not mentioned in the law of 1647, though its use in a minor capacity was implied.

Tuition was the sole source of support, doubtless, in the private schools that existed. There is only one of these, however, which received such recognition from the town and colony that it may

---

[1] Boston Recs. II. pp. 65, 82.
[2] Dorchester Recs., pp. 39, 104.
[3] Dedham Recs., III. pp. 92, 105.
[4] Deare Island was rented for £7 a year.
[5] Frothingham, Charleston p. 115.

be regarded in any sense as a town school. This was Elijah Corlett's school at Cambridge. His entire income before 1648, when a grant of land was made him, came from tuition fees.[1]

Endowment as a source of support was a thing feasible only in the future. Dorchester in her " rules and orders " made provision for a " school stock whether the same be in land or otherwise, both such as is already in being and such as may by any good means hereafter be added."[2] The demands of a new colonial enterprise and the hard times during the first few years of the fifth decade precluded the possibility of any of this kind of " stock " at this time. There is no mention of anything that would correspond to an annuity from the crown. This English method could not in the nature of things exist.

It thus appears, so far as the records furnish evidence, that practically the only method copied in the town schools from English practice was support from land, and this at best furnished but a small part or none at all of the master's salary in these towns where it was instituted.[3] The custom of setting apart land for the school persisted however for many years. Later, endowment created some revenue as well. These were never sufficient however to pay the master's salary. Income from a school stock forms a constant factor in school support during the entire period of this study. But as it had no effect upon the information of the moving school, it needs no further attention than is necessary to keep the fact of its existence before us. It is the manner in which the balance, and the greater amount passed through its evolution that needs to be considered.

The question is, how did the Puritans raise this balance, the greater part of the whole. Obviously, to answer it fairly we must pursue our inquiry on a parallel with the development of church support. That is, the time before 1639 or 1640 must be separated from the years which follow because of the transition from the contribution to the compulsory contribution in maintaining the ministry, and to a lesser extent in building the churches and aiding the poor.

Before proceeding it will be of value to define the terms contribution and compulsory contribution as they will be used in

---

[1] Cambridge Recs., p. 77.   Paige. Cambridge, p. 367.
[2] Dorchester Recs,. p. 55.
[3] Salem records make no reference to land for the use of the school.

connection with school support. By a contribution is meant a donation or subscription of money or goods made to the support of a public enterprise without the pressure of an ultimate legal compulsion in the event of failure to so do. By a compulsory contribution is meant a donation or subscription made under such pressure. This compulsory contribution was often spoken of by the Puritan as "voluntary." This was because it was fundamentally a subscription to which at first all who desired paid the amounts they wished. Afterward the rate was resorted to to bring up the deficiencies. The term "voluntary" was introduced and emphasized, in all probability, in order to put the best face upon it to those who were not readily inclined to give. There would be good warrant for calling this latter development, the "voluntary contribution," but it contains obvious disadvantages.

There is only one instance in the records of the use of the contribution before 1640—that in Boston in 1636. This was a subscription made in a meeting of the "richer inhabitants" "towards the maintenance of a free school master for the youth with us"—that is, for all the children of the town. The list of subscribers is headed by the Governor, the Deputy Governor, the ex-deputy Governor, the colonial treasurer, and the selectmen. These colonial and town officers often co-operated at this early time. The movement is on the face seen to be one undertaken by the selectmen—the town's officials—for the good of its citizens, at a time when there was little system in affairs of government, and when institutions had not been differentiated. A school was wanted, it mattered little to them how the money was to be secured. None of the customs they had known in England could avail here, and some other had to be chosen. The range of the subscription indicates the presence of men of widely varying degrees of wealth. The Governor and Deputy Governor each gave ten pounds, one man gave forty shillings; another, thirty; six, twenty; two, thirteen shillings four pence; seven, ten shillings; two, eight shillings; five, six shillings eight pence; one, six shillings; five, five shillings; seven, four shillings; three, one shilling. There were forty-five subscriptions in all, which must be considered, as conditions were at that time, a large number.

It was undoubtedly intended by them that the school should be open to all, though they were just as certainly conscious of the fact that the action was not taken in town meeting and that legally the town had not participated in the action.   Yet the enterprise was sufficiently of a public nature for the record of it to be given a place in the back of the town record book.   On this point two things are to be said: First, that the school support evidently did not seem to be a proper subject for town legislation.   Second, that the newness of the enterprise, the enthusiasm for its success, tended to produce spontaneous gatherings such as this where the more well-to-do could give in large amounts and those less able, to the extent of their ability.[1]

The records of the other towns during these first few years of the life of the colony say nothing whatever about support. Taken alone no decision can be reached.   Can it be asserted, that, because they say nothing, the method used in the only instance of which there is record, was used in all or in many others?   Obviously not, yet there is some value in this consideration.

Let us consider the possible methods that might have been used.   These were income from land, endowment, tuition, town rate, and contribution.   Had proceeds from land been used it would have first been necessary for the land to have been set apart for this purpose by the town meeting.   Although town records are meagre on some points, this is the one on which they are the most full.   They contain no such record.   It is, therefore, a fair conclusion, that this was not a source of support for the master.   Endowment at this early time could not in the nature of things have existed.   It, also, can, therefore, be disregarded.

Tuition was then used in Eaton's private school at Cambridge. It was doubtless the chief source of support for all private schools.   Could it have been the manner of supporting town schools as well during these first few years of the settlement? This question must be answered in the affirmative; it might have been.   The plan of tuition could be carried on without any town record.   But is it probable?   There is in its favor the

---

[1] Boston Recs. II. p. 8.   At the town meeting when the building of the fortification on Fort Hill was provided for, just eight months previous, all were given a certain amount of work to do; but the richer were to pay money in addition, and the poor were to be paid for some of their labor.   Twelve of these same men "lent" £5 each.

acquaintance of the Puritan with the system in the English schools and in the private schools in the colony. There is also the possibility that the town took over the private school into its own control using the same method of support, as was done frequently in the latter part of the century. Let us examine these considerations more closely. Why should the town establish a school at this time? It was not required to do so by colonial law. It was primarily because the necessity of an education for all was one of the essentials, as they conceived it, of the perpetuity of their social-religious order. A school was needed to which all children might go, whether they were able to pay tuition or not. If the town required tuition of those who could pay, it was necessary to raise the tuition of the poor children in some other way. Tuition could not have been the sole source of support; it might have been required of those whose parents were able to pay.

But there are certain considerations that may be urged against it. Tuition rests upon the principle of the obligation of the parent to educate his own child. It is individualistic in essence. Society in Massachusetts at this time was, on the contrary, tending in the opposite direction—to communism. The altruistic spirit was being manifested in a manner which was unusual in the world's civilization as it existed at that time. People gave freely, in so far as they were able, to the general good. They did not insist on personal rights and personal obligations. They were interested in the welfare of their neighbor's children as well as their own; and even to the extent of being willing to pay to the support of the school not according to their direct benefit, but according to their ability to give to a public measure. This was the case in other public enterprises and in one town school at least; it might have been universally the case in the support of schools. Tuition does not seem fully compatible with this kind of society, because it is individualistic and selfish in its essence. Nevertheless, it might have been used in some towns. Its use must be considered as probable.

The town rate payable in money was in use at this time for defraying certain common charges as those for the herding of cattle,[1] for the erecting of fences and building of bridges,[2] for

---

[1] Boston Recs. II. p. 2. Dorchester Recs. p. 11.
[2] Dorchester Recs. II. p. 4.

fortifications,[1] for highways [2] and for erecting a meeting house.[3]   But it was not used so often as it is natural in this day to assume.   Their needs were neither frequent nor great.   Such rates as there were, were for purely civil purposes.   The amounts, moreover, were small, so that a rate for the master's salary would have seemed a tremendous burden.   Thus there is nothing in the use then made of the town rate to lead us to expect that it was used for a purpose that was strongly religious in its source. And when is added the further consideration that " in history nothing proceeds from nothing," taking into account that a public tax had never been levied in England for support of schools, it seems beyond the bounds of possibility.   Some other method must have intervened between the English methods and the town rate in a normal historical evolution of institutions.

Of these four possibilities—the first two may be thrown out of all consideration.[4]   The third—tuition—may be admitted with a fair degree of probability.   The same may be said of the fourth—the town rate—but with a considerable further limitation as to the degree of its probable use.   But neither satisfy all the conditions in the situation.

The fifth possible method of school support, the contribution, satisfies the early social conditions which tuition and the town rate failed to meet.   It well exemplifies the self-sacrificing communal spirit which pervaded society at that time.   All of the people were held close together in a common brotherhood centering in the church which enforced the teachings of the Bible in the daily life.   Men gave to the common cause with an unusual degree of freedom to all the projects that were deemed necessary to the welfare of the church and state.   Likewise the newness of the enterprise fostered general giving from all who were able.   Also, the contribution is in agreement with the principle governing school support as expressed in the Welsh Education Act of 1649.   This act being a fair expression of the Puritan attitude toward the school and its support, it is therefore most reasonable to expect that it was in general use in many towns.

---

[1] Dorchester Recs. II. pp. 5, 7.
[2] Watertown, Recs. p. 8.
[3] Ibid, p. 1.
[4] They both came into use at a later period, the former—income from land—within year or two after the compulsory contribution came into use.

Finally, the contribution has also this in its favor. For the first time the school was an institution in which the entire social group was interested, but it was not yet regarded as a project which the civil power should support. Throughout all history enterprises of general social interest which the state does not take up are supported by contribution of the inhabitants. Such was the case in the support of the early Christian church and of the church in England during the early centuries of its history, as well. The poor in the mother country had been supported in the same manner. When the state undertook the support of these institutions it gradually brought to bear the compelling power of a legal process. As will be seen in the latter part of this chapter and in chapter three, the support of the school in Massachusetts passed through the later stages of this process. It is, therefore, fair to presume that the contribution was in general use during these earlier years.

Thus, even if there was but one recorded instance of the contribution reason would lead to the conclusion that it was the method most likely to have been followed in those cases where the records are silent, because it satisfies the political, social, and ecclesiastical conditions which were existent in the colony at that time, and because it corresponds to the stage of development in which the school was at that time. Nevertheless, tuition might have been adopted in some towns.

Let us now examine the records of these first few years in these other towns to determine as definitely and accurately as we may whether tuition or the contribution was used. Final judgment must be deferred, however, until the records of the next sub-period, from 1639 to 1647, are examined. In this period the workings of the compulsory contribution are more apparent, and thus it will be possible to form a more satisfactory judgment after the whole period is studied.

The act of the town of Charleston in 1636: "Mr. William Witherell was agreed with to keep a school for a twelve months to begin the eighth of August and to have £ 4s this year." Here is a legislative act which is unusually complete and yet which does not specify the manner in which the amount was to be raised. Had they had a town rate in mind it would most certainly have been inserted; had they intended that tuition was to be charged, which as has been seen is not probable for social reasons, the rate would have very probably been specified, but if the contribution was to be depended upon there was no reason whatever for saying anything about the amounts which anyone should pay. That was a personal rather than a civil affair. Thus, this instance offers confirmatory evidence of the existence of the contribution in another town.

The note on the records of Ipswich which states that in 1636, " a grammar school is set up, but does not succeed " makes either tuition or the contribution possible, or both.

The record of 1636 in Boston is the strongest evidence that the contribution was used in 1635. The wording of the records of the earlier year contains, however, good internal evidence of this view. The fact that Mr. Philemon Pormont was " intreated " to become schoolmaster indicates the respect shown the person of the master and suggests the close relationship between the Pastor and the Master expressed in the Welsh Education Act of 1649, wherein it is evident that the Puritan Parliament " regarded a schoolmastership as an appointment that ranked with a benefice." The support of the schoolmaster was provided from the same fund.[1]

Felt in his *Annals of Salem* states that the first schoolmaster there " was the Rev. John Fisk who appears to have commenced his duties...... in 1637 " and that " Besides teaching he assisted Mr. Peters in the pulpit, and so continued over two years." The most satisfactory explanation of his method of support is that of the contribution, for this statement likewise suggests the same relationship as that just referred to in Boston and the possibility of the same source of support. The decision depends upon whether it was regarded as a town or private school. If it were the latter, tuition was probably used.

Finally, it is to be said that there are no records which do not permit the possibility that the contribution was used, except in the distinctly private grammar school in Cambridge; that all other records, except that of Ipswich in 1636, indicate on their face greater probability that the contribution was used; that in the case of Ipswich judging by the wording of the records above, contribution and tuition are equally probable; that in Charleston in 1636, in Boston in 1635 the contribution was almost certainly

---

[1] De Montmorency, State Intervention, p. 101.

used and in Salem also in 1637-9, if the school was a town school; and that in Boston in 1636, it certainly prevailed. This evidence of the records combined with our knowledge of the ideals of society at that time and the later evolution of school support seems to indicate the general prevalence of the contribution, and that there was no doubt of its dominance over all the English methods of support of the time, including tuition. Our final conclusion must be reserved, however, until after a study of the records during the period of the compulsory contribution to which we now proceed.

The sub-period from 1638 to 1647 is marked at the beginning by the enactment of the compulsory contribution and at the close by the passage of the first law regarding schools. It furnishes more full and definite information and for that reason throws additional light upon the practices of the previous years. It is to be borne in mind that our inquiry seeks to ascertain how that part of the master's support, of whatever proportion, which was not afforded by income from land and endowment, was provided for. In the previous period there was no record making any mention whatsoever of these sources of support; in this, Boston, Dorchester and Charleston obtain some revenue in these ways.[1] The possible methods for raising this balance are the town rate, tuition, and either form of the contribution. That which has been said of them in connection with the previous years holds true in the main here. However, the altruistic spirit of the people was moderating, and the economic straits brought about by the ceasing of immigration in the early forties and associated causes made liberal giving to the public welfare more difficult. This would operate in favor of greater probability of the use of the rate and tuition. But the compulsory contribution contained in itself the coercive element in both tuition and the town rate, and so it would be reasonable to expect that their use would not be so general as might at first thought be supposed. Let us now proceed to the examination of the records, taking first those wherein definite methods are named.

Boston by 1644 was working the compulsory contribution in full force. This is evidenced by an account given in Win-

---

[1] See Appendix A.

throp's History of New England under date of 1645, and which was written, probably, under the impulse of the foundation of the "Free School in Roxburie" in that year. He says, "Divers free schools were erected as at Roxbury . . . . . . and at Boston (where they made an order to allow fifty pounds to the master and an house, and thirty pounds to an usher, who shall also teach to read and write and cipher, and Indian children were to be taught freely, and the charge to be yearly by contribution, either by voluntary allowance, or by rate of such as refused etc., and this order was confirmed by the General Court). Other towns did the like providing maintenance by several means." [1]　A record of a selectmen's meeting in the previous year shows that the practice was in use then also,—" It is ordered that the constables shall pay into Deacon Eliot [a selectman] for the use of Mr. Woodbridge eight pounds due him for keeping the school the last year." [2]　It is evident that the selectmen were estimating roughly the amount each man should contribute, using as a basis the levy made by them of country and town rates,[3] and that the constable was collecting from those who did not freely give an amount approximately proportionate to their share. It cannot be determined how long the compulsory contribution was in use before 1644. It is clear however that it is the lineal descendant of the contribution as made in 1636. And it may be assumed as a historical fact that they were the only methods used in Boston during all the history of the town school to 1645.

The law of 1638 developed two tendencies in its application. The above account of the Boston practice illustrates perfectly one of them—the payment of every inhabitant to the support of school according to "his estates and with consideration of all other his abilities." [4]　But whether it was the intention of the framers of the law or not, its wording permits another interpretation, the realization of which represents the second tendency. The clause which declared "that every inhabitant in any town is liable to contribute to all charges, both in church and commonwealth, whereof he doth, or may receive benefit," may be interpreted as imposing the coercive power of the compulsory contribution only upon those who had children of school age.

(1) Winthrop, Hist. of N. E. II. p. 264.
(2) Boston Recs. II. p. 82.
(3) Ibid, pp. 61-2.
(4) Act of 1634. Mass. Col. Recs. I. p. 120.

The former was a step in the direction of the town rate, the latter a step toward a tax " on the heads of scholars," or tuition-tax.

The act of Salem in 1644 illustrates this second tendency. But there was of necessity in this act another element as well. It was a Puritan principle that all children should have an elementary education. This principle was crystallized into the law of 1642, and, while it did not require the establishment of schools, yet it undoubtedly had that tendency, for it must have been the easiest solution of the problem for some towns. However that may be, if the Puritans had a town school, it must be open to all the children of the town. This being the case, the question arose what men should pay for the instruction of the poor children, if the voluntary subscription should be paid only by those who had children. Here the people of Salem fell back upon English practice as regards the support of the poor, and which they had begun to carry out in the aid of their own poor during the previous year—the levying of a town rate. The act as passed therefore provided,—" Ordered that a vote be published on the next lecture day that such as have children to be kept at school, would bring in their names and what they will give for one whole year, and, also, that if any poor body hath children or a child, to be put to school and not able to pay for their schooling, that the town will pay for it by a rate." Although this was not, it will be seen, strictly the tuition system, yet it was an approach toward it. It was, however, the town rate, and it is the first town rate that was ever levied, so far as the records tell us, for a town school. And it is significant to note, that it was for the benefit of the children of the poor.

This record in itself would indicate an approach toward a system of tuition enforced by the town, rather than a departure from it. If this be true, then it is probable that tuition had not been used previously in the support of the town master. The pastor-master of 1637 was probably supported by the contribution. The record of the action of 1640 indicates its probable continuance. The economic conditions of the intervening years are sufficient to account for the change.

This is the only record of the period illustrating the second tendency of the compulsory contribution. It is represented in the law of 1647. and in the last fifty years of the century its two

3

elements existed in combination in most of the towns of the Commonwealth. The other towns showing the first tendency will next be taken up.

In 1645, the inhabitants of Dedham at a general town meeting " did with unanimous consent declare by vote their willingness to promote that work [education of youth] promising to put to their hands to provide maintenance for a free school in our said town.........And further did resolve and consent testifying it by vote to raise the sum of twenty pounds per annum towards the maintaining of a schoolmaster." In the event however that income from the school land makes the payment of this sum unnecessary, then " every man may be proportionably abated by his sum of the said £20 aforesaid freely to be given to ye as aforesaid."[1]

The " voluntary " feature is apparent, they all " did with unanimous consent declare......their willingness " each to pay his share of twenty pounds; the same " freely to be given." Such is the outline in brief. It was a legal town meeting. Their act established a town school, determined the amount that should be annually spent, and fixed the manner in which the amount should be raised. It imposed also a compulsory contribution upon all the inhabitants. It is interesting to note that emphasis was placed upon the fact that all men bound themselves by the action, as if this was necessary to effect payment of the sums " freely to be given." The controlling thought seems to have been, in respect to this feature of support, that a solemn agreement was formed between them each to do his part, and that the business should be so carried out as to make every one feel the seriousness of his obligation. The thought of the power of the town to levy a tax which would effect this same arrangement seems not to have existed, even though the action was taken in town meeting. On the other hand, the fact that a majority of the meeting were in favor of having a town school doubtless did have considerable effect in producing the unanimity recorded. For it was evident to all that if a majority passed the legislation to have a school, they would be obliged by the law of 1638 to pay their approximate shares whether they agreed or not, and it was better for them to express their willingness irrespective of their true state of mind. The transitional character of the act is evident.

---

[1] Dedham Recs. III. p. 105.

In the setting that has thus far been created in this chapter, the action of the inhabitants of Roxbury in 1645 does not seem to be out of place. While on the one hand it seems a reproduction of the English chartered school with such adaptation as the new environment rendered necessary, yet looked at from the point of view from which the people regarded their own act it seems to contain a distinctly Puritan element in so far as the support of the master was concerned. Its consideration will be of value in this study. A close scrutiny of the provisions of its " charter " will aid not only in determining the relative place of the different methods of support, but also in giving us a fuller appreciation of what the compulsory contribution was.

The covenant entered into by all, or practically all, of the inhabitants of Roxbury in 1645 created simply a perpetual compulsory contribution. After the preamble the agreement continues, —" They therefore unanimously have consented and agreed to erect a free school...... and to allow twenty pounds per annum to the schoolmaster, to be raised out of the Messauges and part of the lands of the several donors........in several proportions as hereafter followeth under their hands................In consideration of the premises, the Donors hereafter expressed for the several proportions or annuities by them voluntarily undertaken and underwritten, have given and granted and by these presents do for themselves their heirs and assigns respectively hereby give and grant unto the present feoffees the several rents and sums hereafter expressed under their hands."[1]

This action is like that of Dedham in the same year except in the point of permanency. The strong emphasis placed on this element caused the Roxbury people to copy after the English chartered school more closely. The adoption of this form of institution removed the source of support from the domain of the civil law, and gave the obligation to support the school an altered sanction. But from the standpoint of its practical effect upon the individuals owning the property at that time or later there was no difference in the two cases. In Dedham each man's " sum " was " freely to be given ; " in Roxbury the " several proportions or annuities " were " voluntarily undertaken." In the former case the civil law obliged each man to pay ; in the

---

[1] Dillaway, Grammar School, pp. 7-13. Brown, Middle Schools, p. 40.

latter the agreement. Both were compulsory " voluntary " contributions, one for an indefinite period of time and subject to variation in amount as the individuals' property changed in value; the other, likewise contained no time limit, but remained fixed in amount and existed as a lien against the piece or pieces of property specified.

These comprise all the records in which the compulsory contribution appears directly. There still remains to be noticed those records of the period which make no explicit reference to it. Such a record is furnished by the town of Dorchester in 1645. The extended rules and orders, which have been several times referred to, provided for a " school stock whether the same be in land or otherwise, both such as is in being and such as may by any good means hereafter be added " and for the payment of the master's salary and " if these be sufficient " the repair of the school house " out of the rents issues and profits " thereof. If there were not sufficient funds for repairing the school house the selectmen were " to tax the town " for that purpose. The entire absence of any mention of taxing the town for the support of the master in this body of regulations which has all the marks of most careful care to secure completeness, taken together with the fact that it could have been easily included in connection with taxing the town for the repair of the school house, is satisfactory evidence that they expected the salary of the master in the event of a shortage in the school stock to be provided for in some other way. That the " school stock " was insufficient to pay the master there is little or no doubt. The rent from Thomson's Island was not sufficient in the early years, and probably remained so.[1]

This balance must have been made up either by tuition charges or by contribution. If tuition had been contemplated it seems that a provision securing it would have been incorporated in this very complete measure, giving the feoffees power to specify the amounts and to collect the same. The fact that their powers were expressly limited to " the charge, oversight and ordering thereof [the school] in such manner as is hereafter expressed " seems conclusive that they could not and did not have anything to do with tuition, and that therefore it was not a means of support. On the other hand their power " to dispose of the

---

[1] Act of 1641. See Appendix A.

school stock......both such as is already in being and such as may by any good means hereafter be added " covers the contribution. It seems therefore practically certain that it was the sole method of support for the balance needed above the income from the permanent part of the " stock."[1]

The records of two other towns remain to be considered. The action of Ipswich in 1642, " that there shall be a free school " permits the interpretation of all forms of support. But as no mention is made of school land, and as the times would hardly permit of an endowment, these may be dismissed at once. Likewise, the town rate, for, as has been shown, to ascribe it at this time would be an anachronism. Tuition and the contribution remain. It is possible that the latter was used, or that tuition was paid by those who were able and the rest was made up by a subscription or by the town rate as a feature of the support of the town. The conditions in Salem, however, would weigh against the fixing of a definite tuition rate. It is impossible to determine the exact method of support.

The school referred to in the records of Newbury was a private school encouraged by public support.[2] There is nothing to indicate that it was regarded as a town school. The master probably got his return from tuition. There were probably other towns who maintained similar relations toward a private school. Elijah Corlett who kept a grammar school in Cambridge for many years received encouragement in the same way. Watertown, is an example of a town, which, judging from the outward conditions, must have had a private school, of which no record remains. The people probably promoted its welfare in many ways.

In addition to the above instances the record of the town of Charleston dated in January 1647, should receive notice. It indicates that a town rate was levied. As the town historian places no confidence in the exact presentation of the records of this time, some doubt is thrown upon whether it was really a town tax that was ordered. The phrase " gathered of the

---

[1] It has been claimed that the action of 1639 was equivalent to laying a tax upon the inhabitants. (Mowry, Address on Schools of Dorchester.) That it was the equivalent of a permanent contribution in the form of a rent by all who chose to take up the portion of land assigned them is seen to be the truth of the matter when viewed in the light of this study. However, the action of two years later made the source of support one of rent of the ordinary kind. The obligation to take their assignment of land and pay the rent was one which could be assumed or not as each choose. Evidently only about seventy of the one hundred and twenty freeholders did so. Rep. Com. of Ed. 1896-7, Note, pp. 1170-71.

[2] Currier, Newbury, p. 395.

town " may be taken as meaning, the voluntary contribution.
This point cannot be fully settled.   Another question is also
involved, whether the date as given is correct. As the date lies
within the first two months of the year, it was, owing to the
method of recording dates, especially liable to error in the compi-
lation that was made.   If the date were January 1648, the town
rate might be more properly conceived as having been levied and
collected, for that would place it in the next period.   This point,
also, must remain unsettled.   It must be said however that it
is possible that the town rate was levied in support of schools
in Charleston in January 1647.   If this were the case, then the
evolution of the contribution with the town rate was worked out
in Charleston without the participation of the General Court in
the process, and the period of the civil school began in this town
at this time.   Under this condition, this act would more properly
be included in the period which followed as it would be if the
action were taken in 1648.

The study of the records of this second sub-period must be
taken as proving conclusively the general prevalence and the
large predominance of the compulsory contribution as a method
of supporting the town schools.   Tuition, on the other hand was
the main source of support of the private schools.   Land and
endowment were not fruitful sources of revenue.   The town
rate was used but once, so far as is known with certainty, and
then as an element in support of the poor altogether as much,
if not more than, as an element in the support of the school.
The well-established dominance of the compulsory contribution
likewise confirms the prevalence of the contribution before 1639.
The most satisfactory solution of the question of support of town
schools is thus afforded by it, though tuition may have been used.
It is, also, plain that its agreement with the social and religious
ideas and practices of the time compels the placing of the burden
of proof upon tuition and the town rate in order to establish
their existence.   The years before 1647 constitute the period of
the contribution in its two forms, the contribution and compulsory
contribution.
Summarizing, it may be said that the Puritan society of this
period was dominantly religious in character ; all of its activities
were closely related to the church, which was the chief institution.

Their principles concerning education were fundamentally religious. The institution—the school—as they had known it in England was closely associated with the Church; their manner of life emphasized this relationship. But owing to the primitive condition of their life the English methods of support could not be used. It became necessary to adopt new methods in order to secure the education of all the children. The methods chosen were the same as those by which the church was supported, and as the methods for the support of the church changed, even so, did the methods for the support of the school. However, methods for the support of the school, since it did not rank so high as the church, were left more to local initiative and regulation.[1]

Taking this period as a whole the people had not as yet fully arrived at the conception of the school as a proper subject for the support of the state though they sought the aid of the state to collect the money. However, as will be seen in the next chapter, they used the civil organization to control the school.

---

[1] The methods for the support of the poor passed through the same evolution and for the same reasons, except that in this line of development there was the influence of a previous evolution, similar in character, which had taken place in England within the preceding century. Thus for this reason, doubtless, the evolution in the case of the support of the poor, preceded that of the support of the school and of the church, and served as an influence in promoting their evolution.

CHAPTER II

CONTROL AND SUPPORT OF THE CHURCH-TOWN SCHOOL [1]

PART II— AGENCIES OF CONTROL

1635-1647

The town meeting as the supreme authority in the control of local affairs could legally create whatever agencies it desired for the execution of its will, and determine their duties and powers both as to extent and duration, subject only to the general supervision of the General Court. In Dorchester in 1645, three feofees appointed by the town for life, but subject to removal, were given the full powers possessed by the town over its school, except in one point—the master selected must be approved by the town. An example of an administrative agency of the opposite extreme in character is found in the same town in 1641, when a committee of two was appointed to perform a single act — the renting of land for the benefit of the school.

The selectmen were the chief administrative agency of the town supplementing the action of the town meeting to whatever extent was necessary or desirable to attain the ends in view. They were elected from time to time, usually annually. Theoretically they were subordinate to the town meeting. They dealt with all features of town government. They constituted an agency, always at hand, which could be used in the accomplishment of any purpose.

In our endeavor to answer the question, which governmental agencies performed the various functions necessary to the establishment and maintenance of a town school, the administrative functions present no difficulty. They were performed by one or another of these administrative agencies — the permanent school committee, the temporary committee, or the selectmen. It is in the consideration of the legislative functions that perplexities arise. There are none, however, when there is a permanent board of feoffees constituted by an instrument, resembling a charter

---

[1] Reference to town records before 1647, all of which are contained in the appendix, are not given in the text.

and of considerable length and detail, for then all is specifically provided for. The same is true in that case in which there was the temporary school committee.[1] But when the selectmen as the "town's representative" and ministerial agent are involved in the control of the school the duties and powers assigned to them are not specified and we are compelled to go beyond the town records to determine whether their actions were confined wholly to the administrative functions. We must know the methods of control of schools as they had existed previously and the nature of the scheme of local government as it was at that time. The same principles of interpretation laid down in the first chapter must be observed here.

The English schools among which the settlers had lived in the mother-country were either chartered or private schools. Full control was placed in a board of feoffees appointed in the charter. Vacancies were filled, likewise, according to its provisions. The so-called town-schools, which present the closest analogy to the town schools in Massachusetts, were chartered, as well, by the crown. The officers of the town government, constituted as feoffees, had their powers and duties determined for them by this legal instrument. Their functions as administrators of the school were outside of their regular official duties. The school was not regarded as a civil institution. It was rather a special institution, whose administration was placed in the town officers in-being, in order to secure obvious advantages for the school. The control in all classes of chartered schools was decidedly aristocratic in character; there was nothing to suggest democratic control." [2]

Puritan theory placed the control of the school in the church organization. This was exemplified in the plan of Knox and his successors in Scotland,[3] and in the Dutch Church in Holland.[4] It was also the plan adopted by the Puritan parliament for Wales in 1649.[5] The Established Church of England during the reign of the kings exercised the right of approval

---

[1] There was only one temporary school committee, dealing directly with the school itself in all towns previous to 1647. This was in Dorchester in 1639, "when it was left to the discretion of the seven men for the time being whether maids shall be taught with the boys or not." The only other temporary committee used for any purpose in connection with school administration was in the same town two years later when the elders were instructed to rent out Thomson's Island.

[2] Stow.

[3] Grant, The Elizabethan Grammar-Schools, , p. 77. *In preparation.*

[4] Monroe, p. 436.

[5] De Montmorency, State Intervention, pp. 101-3.

or disapproval of the masters of all the schools of whatever kind.[1] The character of the control that the Puritans in Massachusetts fixed upon for the school must have been influenced in large measure by the ideas prevalent throughout the church at that time. This requires a study of the form of church government.

The Calvinistic government was a peculiar combination of aristocracy and democracy. Fundamentally democratic in theory, the limitations placed upon the range of action of the congregation were so close that the Elders had theoretically, and often in practice, almost complete control. The relation of these two bodies in the church is set off clearly and authoritatively in a volume of the Rev. Richard Mather of Dorchester.[2]

" We do believe that Christ hath ordained that there should be a Presbytery or Eldership......whose work is to teach and rule the Church by the word and laws of Christ, and under whom so teaching and ruling all the people ought to be obedient and submit themselves." To the congregation as a whole " Christ hath given to them [liberty] in choosing their own officers, in admitting of members, and censuring of offenders even Ministers themselves when they be such. We give the exercise of all church power of government neither all to the people excluding the Presbytery nor all to the Presbytery excluding the people. For this were to make the government of the church either merely democratical, or merely aristocratical, neither of which we believe it ought to be." The elders could do nothing without the consent of the people, " because when they do their duty, the people ought to consent to it and ' if any man should in such case wilfully dissent, the Church ought to deal with such an one, for not consenting ' or else ' they shall all be guilty of the sinful dissent of such an one ' ".....Church matters ought not to be determined " merely by multitude or plurality of votes, but by rules from the Word of Christ whose will (and not the major or minor part of men) is the only rule and law for Churches." The rules of Christ were to be determined by the Elders. Thus the rule of the Elders was theoretically absolute. They possessed the power of nullifying the votes of all dissenters. In practice this was modified to some extent by the influence of the

---

[1] De Montmorency, p. 96.
[2] Quoted by Dexter, Congregationalism, p. 427.

ministry on the one hand and of the congregation on the other. However, the ministry and Elders were usually in close agreement, and more often than not at this early time, the people were swayed by the Elders in the exercise of the powers that were specifically confirmed to them. The government was in reality " a speaking aristocracy in the form of a silent democracy."[1]

Thus both English practice and Puritan theory predisposed the Puritan to aristocratic control of the school. But there was another element in the situation — the local civil organization. It has been said that they were a practical people, that they cared not so much for the character of the means as for the accomplishment of the ends in view. The custom of the past or present would be quickly modified if a better result would follow. So when the Puritan faced the question of the selection of the best method of controlling the school he was ready to modify the old ideas and practices of the chartered school and of the church school, if the end could be attained more directly and economically by town control.

The extent to which the old models were copied in school support was very large; in methods of control it was far less. The Roxbury Grammar School was modelled most closely after the English chartered schools. The " Rules and Orders " for the school in Dorchester, passed in 1645, shows this influence to a large degree also. Records of other towns manifest the effects of the English practice to a lesser degree. There were no schools modeled after the strictly church school, except possibly the school kept by Rev. John Fish in Salem in 1637-9, when he assisted Mr. Peters in the pulpit.[2] There was no need for them. The civil government had the machinery already at hand. Church and State were in very close union or alliance. Why create additional administrative organs in the church, when the town agencies would suffice? And so the civil organization was chosen in many of the towns to control the school for the reason that it offered the most direct method. And thus unconsciously the control of the school was transferred from the church to the state.

[1] Dexter, Congregationalism, p. 429.
[2] Felt Salem I. p. 427. Newbury in the latter part of the century had a similar arrangement for pastoral services. In this case, of course, the teacher was hired by the town. Currier's Newberry, p. 401.

The town government was in a formative stage.[1]   The people did not have a body of practice to guide them in civil affairs, and they had to work out a form of government without further precedent than the English parish.   The form of government used in the churches was the most fruitful source of influence.   However, because of the numerous secular and property interests involved in town business, the democratic features of the church government were most strongly emphasized. Town citizenship was much broader than colonial citizenship: and the head local officers were not kept in their position for so long a period of time.   Nevertheless at this early time, when the church was the primary institution in the town settlements and civil agencies of government were in a formative stage, the aristocratic features of the church government must have exercised a strong influence upon the civil practice.

After this review of the external conditions which were influencing the inhabitants of the towns in the control of their schools we are prepared to go on more intelligently with an interpretation of the town records. Our question has now been reduced to this form:— In those towns where the school was controlled wholly by the town meeting and the selectmen to what extent did each agency enter into the performance of the legislative functions? Let us first take those instances in the records wherein it is clear that the town meeting performed all or nearly all the necessary legislative functions. They are as follows:

Charleston 1636,— " Mr. William Mitchell was agreed with to keep a school for a twelve month to begin the eighth of August and to have £45 this year."

Dorchester — " It is ordered that there shall be a rent of £20 yearly forever imposed on Thomson's Island — toward the maintenance of a school......the said schoolmaster to be chosen from time to time by the freemen."

Salem 1643 — " Ordered that a vote be published on the next lecture day that such as have children to be kept at school, would bring in their names and what they will give for one whole year, and also that if any poor body hath children or a

---

[1] Hosmer, Samuel Adams, the Man of the Town Meeting; also his Samuel Adams, p. 3.

child to be put to school and not able to pay for their schooling, that the town will pay for it by a rate."[1]

Dedham 1645: "The said inhabitants......for the education of youth in our said town did with an unanimous consent declare by vote their willingness to promote that work......And further did resolve......by vote to raise the sum of twenty pounds per annum towards the maintaining of a schoolmaster......and also......to betrust the said twenty pounds per annum and certain lands in our town......into the hands of feoffees...... that as the profits shall arise from ye said land every man may be proportionately abated of his sum of the said twenty pounds aforesaid freely to be given to ye use aforesaid."

The various necessary legislative functions were (1) decision to have a school; (2) election of master; (3) determination of how master should be paid; (4) determination of amount to be paid him or the length of the term of school.[2]   In Charleston the town meeting failed to cover the third point; in Salem and Dedham the second point.

The records which reveal quite incomplete legislation upon the part of the town are:

Boston 1635: "Likewise it was then generally agreed upon that our brother Philemon Pormont shall be intreated to become schoolmaster for the teaching and nurturing of children with us."

Salem 1640 — "Young Mr. Norris chose by this assembly to teach school."

Ipswich 1642 — "The town votes that there shall be a free school."

It may be assumed that in each case the first function was performed.[3]   The second function was not performed in Ipswich; the third and fourth are lacking in all of them.

Now let us look at these records with the point of view of determining whether any legislative action was necessary in those years where none was recorded.   In Boston there is no record of legislative action concerning the school proper from 1635 until after the close of the period.   Yet the action of the inhabi-

---

[1] The Charleston record of 1647 is not included because logically, and probably also in fact, it belongs to the next period.

[2] See page 13.

[3] Though in the case of Salem, where we know there was a school previously taught by the Rev. John Fish while serving as an assistant in the pulpit, it is not certain.   The decision to have a school may have previously been declared by the town meeting or the selectmen, and the action be merely the fulfilling of the second function.

tants in 1636, the setting apart of Deare Island for the benefit
of the school or other public purpose in 1642, and the act of
the selectmen ordering the master paid a small amount in 1644,
as well as the deep intellectual and religious interests centering
in Boston indicate beyond a doubt the continuous existence of
the school. The schools of Salem and Ipswich are also said
to have been continuous from the date of the first town records.[1]
There is no reason to believe that the same was not true of the
schools of Dorchester and Charleston as well.[2]   If so, was
it then necessary that any of these legislative functions be
performed?

In the act of Dorchester in 1639 the continuous existence
of the school was implied; in Charleston on the other hand its
duration was definitely limited to one year. What interpretation
is to be placed upon the records of those towns in which the
decision to have a school is not given any time limit? As the
chief factor of the school was the master and as his office was
regarded as being similar to that of a pastor, who was elected
for an indefinite time, it might be presumed that the decision
to have a school continued during the life of the master or the
period that the town and the master were willing to have the
relationship continue.[3]   Judging on this basis it became necessary for Boston to perform this first function several times for
we know that besides Mr. Pormont, Mr. Daniel Maud, Mr.
Woodbridge, and possibly Mr. Woodmansey served as school-
mster before 1648.[4]   Proceeding on the same basis, we would
be led to say that Salem was not compelled to pass upon this
question, for Mr. Norris seems to have been the master in 1668
and 1673 and probably during all the intervening time. But
there is strong reason for believing that the action of 1640 was
not so meant. For in the following year the Quarterly Court
ordered a town meeting in Salem to consider the question of a
free school.[5]   If our conclusion in the first chapter that the
school of 1640 was such, be true, the interpretation to be put
upon the act of the Court is that the people of Salem were
hesitating whether to continue it. The record of Ipswich may

---

(1) Felt, Salem, p. 429. Felt, Ipswich, Essex and Hamilton, p. 87.
(2) Barnard's American Journal of Education, XVI. p. 105, XXVII. p. 127.
(3) See Dorchester Recs, 1642—Memorandum—Appendix.
(4) Boston Recs. II. pp. 82, 99.
(5) Felt, Salem, p. 427.

be interpreted in either way. Thus it seems that in some towns this first necessary legislative function was performed and not recorded.

Performance of the second legislative function—the election of a master—must have occurred in all the above cases, and also in Dorchester whenever the first and the succeeding master's services came to an end. The " acts and orders " of 1645 in their provision for the election of master imply some change in the office.

In the discussion of the third and fourth points of necessary legislation those records where legislation is only partial may be included. Our question is, whether the manner of raising the master's salary was a necessary legislative function in those years when no mention of it is made in the records. It was noted in the previous chapter that no mention whatever was made of the manner of raising the master's salary until 1639, and that when the question was passed upon in town meetings after that date the methods provided were chiefly income from land and voluntary contribution, though provision was made (in Dorchester), whereby gifts would be received and (in Salem) a tax was levied for the education of poor children.

The fact that there was no legislation upon this point before 1639 is explained by the nature of school support up to that time. The contribution was accepted as the proper means and there was no need for legislation. However, when the compulsory contribution had to be resorted to in order to have a school, legislation to secure its enforcement in each town became necessary. This time came in Boston as early as 1644, in Salem as early as 1643, in Dedham as early as 1645 and possibly earlier in the first two towns. Although it is possible that in some towns, as in Ipswich and Charleston and Dorchester, they continued to use the contribution, yet it is more likely that the compulsory contribution was adopted in the first two for part of this time. In Boston there is no record of this action ever being taken, in Salem and Dedham for only one year. In the last town the action may be taken as extending over a period of years, but not in Salem. Thus it is certain that in some of the towns, and probably in most of them, legislation was passed upon this point of which no record of the usual form was made.

As to the fourth point—the fixing of the master's salary—there are only two records which fix it definitely over a period of years — in Dorchester in 1639, and in Dedham in 1645. In the former instance we know that the source of income was a disappointment, and it seems very probable that it was necessary to change the amount. The frequency with which legislation was necessary was dependent principally upon the economic status, the constancy of the income from land and other sources, and the length of time a master when once elected would serve. If a change should occur in either of these points, a modification in the amount of the master's salary would undoubtedly become a subject of legislation. Changes in all these respects we know to have occurred during this period, and so we can conclude with reasonable certainty that this subject was frequently a subject of legislation in all the towns.

Summarizing our inquiry into the question of unrecorded legislation we conclude that there must have been a considerable amount in each of the towns. It does not seem too much to say that in the majority of towns it was greater in amount than that which was recorded. This has been seen to be true of Boston, Ipswich after 1642, and Charleston. In Salem there is recorded legislation in only two years out of eight, in Dorchester in two out of six, which facts indicate the truth of the assertion in them as well. In Dedham, on the other hand, this condition hardly prevailed. Furthermore, the legislation that remained unrecorded seems to have been fully equivalent in rank to that which appears in the town records. Upon every point there seems to have been need for legislation during the interims.

Now if this be true, the conclusion seems to follow inevitably that the selectmen passed the far greater portion of this legislation. This view recognizes the possibility of action by town meeting failing of record, some instances of which must have existed, e. g., the town meeting ordered at Salem by the Court of Quarter Sessions in 1641. But to insist that this would be true of a large number of instances is hardly in accord with the inherent probabilities of the records themselves or with the conditions prevalent in the political and social life. This view is supported by the following considerations:—

(1) The selectmen possessed equivalent powers with the town meeting in respect to schools. The board of selectmen began to assume pretty definite form by 1640. In the "Body of Liberties," passed in 1641 by the General Court, the institution was given its permanent form. This provided that, "The free-men of every town or township shall have full power to choose yearly or for less time out of themselves a convenient number of fit men to order the planting or prudential occasions of the town according to instructions given them in writing. Provided nothing be done contrary to the public laws and orders of the country, provided also the number of such select persons be not over nine."[1]

The towns as a rule at this time passed upon the instructions in the general town meeting held for the election of officers. Watertown in 1634 "agreed by the consent of the freemen that these eleven freemen shall order all the civil affairs for the town for the year following, and to divide the lands."[2] In 1641, the wording was "to order the town affairs;" in 1647 "to order the prudential affairs of the town."[3] The authority of the Boston town meeting in 1634 was conveyed by the phrase "to manage the affairs of the town."[4] In 1636, ten men were "with general consent, chosen for these next six months to oversee and set order for all allottments belonging to the town, and for all other occasions and businesses of the same (excepting matters of election for the General Court) from time to time to be agreed upon and ordered by them or the greater part of them."[5]

In 1639 the ten men were "chosen as formerly for the town's occasions." Dedham in 1639 "concluded that whatever power all ye company of townsmen themselves so met together before any such choice was now made, the very same power is now put into the same men's hands now chosen to remain in full power for one whole year from the present day." [6] Dorchester in 1633 did not enter fully into representative government and limited the acts of its "ten men" by a sort of referendum, although they were privileged to act upon all subjects.[7] By

---

(1) Whitmore, Colonial Laws, p. 49.
(2) Watertown Recs. I. p. 2.
(3) Ibid I. pp. 7, 10.
(4) Boston Recs. II. p. 2.
(5) Ibid II. p. 11.
(6) Dedham Recs. III. 62.
(7) Dorchester Recs. 3.

4

1639, this form of control had ceased to exist and the " seven men " were empowered " to order all the affairs of the plantation, and to have full power to act and determine anything for the good of the plantation according to their discretion, except in granting land." [1]   In Salem no specific instructions were given, but they were called the " town's representatives " in 1636, which implies these same full powers as in other towns.   In 1638 they were called the " seven men appointed for the town's affairs." [2]

While none of the instructions of the towns contain specific reference to the subject of schools, yet there is no doubt that these were included in them.   A law passed in 1647, dealing with the powers of those, who, although not being church members, were admitted to the privileges of citizenship in the town, makes this plain.   In this law some of the chief " prudentials proper to ye selectmen " are named.   The " ordering of schools " is given the first place followed by the " herding of cattle, laying out of highways and distributing of lands." [3]   There is no doubt that legally they had full power to perform these legislative functions.

(2) That they exercised powers equivalent to those of the town meeting in other affairs is evident to the student of the records. Howard in his *Local Constitutional History of the United States* speaks as follows upon this point: " As the town representative a vast number of functions devolved upon the selectmen.   Nearly every kind of business that could be transacted by the town meeting itself, save only the election of the more important officers, was constantly performed by them.   Their proceedings were recorded by the town clerk, usually in the same book and interspersed with those of the town meeting.   Indeed the minutes of the former are scarcely to be distinguished in character and form from those of the latter body." [4]

(3) The charter of school administration previous to that time was aristocratic.   The point needs no further elaboration here. The natural tendency would have been to place the control of the school in the hands of a few men.   It was done in Dorchester and in Dedham in 1645, and in Roxbury also, though this was not properly a town school.   The natural tendency expressed here must have operated also in the other towns.

[1] Dorchester Recs. p. 38.
[2] Salem Recs. pp. 15, 77.
[3] Mass. Col. Recs. II. p. 197.
[4] Howard, p. 78.

(4) The fact that the school was in a period of transition from an institution of the church to an institution of the state emphasized aristocratic control. To the Puritan the school belonged primarily to the church, and thus subject to aristocratic control. The peculiar situation which brought about its control by the civil organization was a mixed situation. Naturally the old forms would not be thrown off at once, and the tendency would be to give pretty full powers to those occupying the highest civil office. Traces of the influences of the old order are seen in the fact that the elders of the church were appointed to perform administrative functions in connection with the school in Dorchester in 1639 and 1641. This influence is apparent later in the employment of Ezekiel Cheever in Boston in 1670; and in the school committee of that town in the eighteenth century.

(5) Absence of records favors action by selectmen. Many of their acts being purely executive in character required no record. This would develop a tendency to laxity in recording which would naturally extend over into acts legislative in character. The conditions under which the legislative action was taken were much more informal than those surrounding the town meeting. This, again, would promote the same tendency.

(6) The contrast in the frequency of town action before and after 1647. The effect of the law of 1647 was to make the people conscious of the fact that the school was a civil institution. In consequence the people were more inclined to assume direct control. Thus after that date record of town action is frequent, while the conditions regarding the school itself were approximately the same. This is illustrated in Dorchester, where we have every reason to believe the school was continuous. Some records as Salem and Boston however continue the same as before, indicating the same method of control. In contrast to the records of these towns are those of Watertown where action is taken annually by the town meeting. From these facts it is reasonable to conclude that if the town had exercised full legislative power over their schools the records of that action would have been made, and that as it does not appear, the selectmen exercised the major portion of the control.

(7) The character of the action of the town when taken shows a favorable disposition toward the selectmen. There is no evi-

dence of interference or restriction upon their executive acts in any way. The whole tendency was toward granting freedom of action. In contrast with this is the evidence of restriction and interference in the succeeding period.

(8) Some towns as Boston and Salem continued the method of large control by the selectmen down into a later period. The records of the selectmen in Boston were written in greater detail at this later time and so we are enabled to study the working of the system as it was carried out in the earlier period. All that can be said here without anticipating a later chapter [1] is to indicate those facts which point to control by the selectmen in this period, leaving the final proof of that fact to the chain of connected events which will be presented in the treatment of the next period. Boston must have at some time assumed the employment of the master in its civil capacity. It must have adopted the voluntary contribution; it must have elected masters on at least two occasions; and it must have determined even more often how much should be raised for the benefit of the school in addition to the income from land, for this varied at different times. There is no evidence of town action at any time. On the other hand the meeting of the richer inhabitants in 1636 was a meeting of all the selectmen and some thirty men in addition which fact points to the activity of the selectmen in this and in later years as well. This alone would point strongly to the selectmen soon assuming full control as officials of the town. But later evidence will fully confirm the fact. [2]

These considerations taken together seem to establish beyond a doubt the conclusion that the selectmen did frequently perform legislative functions without specific instructions from the town. They acted as the " town's representative," by virtue of the broad powers bestowed upon them in town meeting. In this respect their position may be compared to that of the Assistants in the colonial government. [3]

Control of schools was thus at times democratic, at times aristocratic, in character. Towns passed from one extreme to another with apparent ease. The two most strongly contrasted methods are found in the same town—Dorchester, in 1639 and

---

[1] Chapter IV.
[2] See pp. 70-1.
[3] Osgood I. pp. 167-8. The analogy between them and the fact that the records of the Assistants have been preserved only in part, strengthens the point in favor of unrecorded legislative action of the selectmen.

1645. This on the one hand indicates the formative stage of civil institutions when democratic and aristocratic tendencies were arrayed against each other, as was the case in the colonial government. On the other hand, it represents the persistence of the old methods of school control and of the working of the Puritan conception of the school as an institution of the church in opposition to secular control of institutions, which was fundamental in their theories of civil government.

It is impossible from the nature of the evidence to determine absolutely which tendency was uppermost. We may judge only from the evidence at hand. It was the period of the permanent school committee or board of feoffees, and of major control of the selectmen in most towns not having the permanent school committee. These indications confirm with reasonable certainty the dominance of aristocratic control. But of this much we may be absolutely certain, *this was the period when the selectmen enjoyed the greatest freedom of control.*

From the standpoint of the agencies of control the school was a civil institution in a church-town. Transition from ecclesiastical to civil control was accomplished by reason of that fact. Yet the character of these agencies was aristocratic like those of the church. From the standpoint of methods of support as was seen in the previous chapter the school was still an institution of the church. It may be best characterized therefore as the church-town school. This term represents the transitional character of the school, the appearance of the new in agencies of control and the persistence of the old in methods of support.

CHAPTER III

CONTROL AND SUPPORT OF THE CIVIL SCHOOL

PART I.— METHODS OF SUPPORT

1647-1700

The passage of the law of 1647 introduced a new epoch in the history of school control and support. In control, the period is to be characterized as bringing about the universal dominance of the democratic *secular* tendency; in the field of support, it is to be marked off as the time of the combined methods of the town rate and tuition rate, or rate on children. The period covers in general the latter half of the seventeenth and the first decades of the eighteenth century. It was also the time when the Puritan first appreciated the fact that the school was a completely civil institution.

At the time of the enactment of the law the town schools, as distinct from the private schools, were controlled largely and generally by a board of feoffees or the selectmen, who exercised equivalent powers. The masters were paid from the proceeds of school " stock," or income from land, and the compulsory contributions. Usually the first two sources of income, when they existed, did not furnish the amount required. It is this balance formerly raised by the compulsory contributions in which this study in concerned.

The law of 1647[1] is often quoted and well known, yet it must again be repeated here:

" It being one of the chief projects of that old deluder Satan to keep men from the knowledge of the Scriptures, as in former times by keeping them in an unknown tongue, so in these latter times by persuading from the use of tongues, that so at least the true sense and meaning of the original might be clouded by false glosses of saint-seeming deceivers, that learning may not be buried in the grave of our fathers in the church and commonwealth, the Lord assisting our endeavors:

" *It is therefore ordered,* That every township in this jurisdiction, after the Lord hath increased them to the number of fifty house-holders, shall then forthwith appoint one within their town

---

[1] Mass. Col. Recs. II. p. 203.

to teach all such children as shall resort to him to write and read, whose wages shall be paid either by the parents or masters of such children, or by the inhabitants in general, by way of supply, as the major part of those that order the prudentials of the town shall appoint: *Provided,* Those that send their children be not oppressed by paying much more than they can have them taught for in other towns; and

" *It is further ordered,* That where any town shall increase to the number of one hundred families or householders, they shall set up a grammar school, the master thereof being able to instruct youth, so far as they may be fitted, for the university: *Provided,* That if any town neglect the performance hereof above one year, that every such town shall pay five pounds to the next school until they shall perform this order."

An analysis of this law from the point of view of its effect upon school control shows:

1st. That it took away from the towns part of the legislative power formerly exercised by them through the town meeting and the selectmen. The legislative powers thus assumed by the General Court were the determination of the questions (a) whether the town should have a school, (b) the length of its term, (c) the kind of a school each town must have and (d) who should be admitted to it.

2nd. That it created a new type of legislation, corresponding to that which was taken away. The voters of each town of fifty householders and over had now to determine, at least annually, through its town meeting or selectmen, whether it would obey the law. Each town had full liberty to decide the question as it chose, although in case of failure it made itself liable to the action of the judicial branch of the colonial government. It was the town's will that was executed in these respects as before, but a changed type of will. It was determined from the point of view of the standard set in the law, rather than from the conception of the people of their own needs.

3rd. That it left with the town the legislative power of determining the amount that should be expended in support of the master. The following clause, " provided, those that send their children be not oppressed by paying much more than they can have them taught for in other towns," was not in reality a limitation to the town. For no town would ever pay more than was necessary to secure a master, and if the least amount for which a master could be had was disproportionate to that paid in other towns, this clause would operate to suspend the law for that town for the time being.

4th. That it left with the towns the legislative power of determining how the master's salary should be raised.

5th. That it did not affect the executive functions as exercised. No mention is made of this class of governmental functions. Each town still had supreme authority within its limits in this regard. There was no state supervision, and none of the town officers were required to execute any expression of the will of the colonial government.

6th. That it did not expressly alter the relations heretofore existing between the organs of local government in their control of schools. It is " the township " or " town " in its corporate capacity that is addressed and held responsible. It was of no consequence which agency of the local government performed the various functions.[1]

An analysis of the law from the point of view of determining its effect upon methods of raising the master's salary shows:—

---

[1] Professor Suzzalo in his monograph on "The Rise of Local School Supervision in Massachusetts", interprets the phrase "those that order the prudentials of the town" as designating the selectmen. To the author its meaning is that either the town meeting or the selectmen could perform the function named, but that it was given to the town meeting primarily as the supreme power in the "town or township," which was held responsible in its corporate capacity for the observance of the law. If the "prudential affair" concerning the support of the master was by the town placed in any other agency, as the selectmen, the "major portion" of those in that office could determine the question.

While the General Court had the power to take away any legislative power it chose from the town meeting where it originally belonged by virtue of its own act of 1634 and to place it exclusively in the hands of the selectmen, yet to have done so would have violated precedent and the Puritan theory of government. The power to tax themselves directly in town meeting or indirectly by specific instructions was a liberty dearly prized and enjoyed throughout the colonial period. Such an interpretation is incongruous with the nature of the Puritan government. That it was not given this meaning is likewise fully demonstrated by the events of future years.

The peculiarity of the expression "those that order the prudential affairs of the town" is of such a nature as to indicate when taken by itself alone that some special organ of government was meant. The use of this language therefore, needs explanation. It was a time when laws were loosely drawn. The legislators wished not to disturb the existing order of administration. In some towns the question of support was determined by town meeting; in others the selectmen had charge, in others still the feoffees raised the funds in both cases by order of the town meeting. At the same time it wished to hold all who composed the town corporation primarily responsible. The term "freemen" would not have sufficed for some non-freemen were entitled to vote in town affairs; the term "inhabitants" would have been too inclusive, for not all of them had the privilege of a voice in the town meeting; the term "freeholders" was inadequate as only residents in the town could vote. The term "those that order the prudential affairs" defined these individuals, and it also permitted the continuance of the existing order of administration in every town. Moreover, the use of the word "inhabitants" in connection with support is exact, for all had to contribute to the support of local affairs whether they had the right of suffrage or not.

Prof. Suzzalo cites this as one of the instances in the evolution of school control by which the powers of the selectmen were continually increased. This interpretation of the course of the evolution is in direct opposition to the view taken in this study. A study dealing with a movement over so long a period of time as Prof. Suzzalo's could not in the limitations of a doctor's thesis take into account other colonial and town records than those which dealt with schools alone. Judging from these records alone his conclusion might seem well founded.

1st. That it did not specifically change the method of support used by any town in the support of its school. It permitted the use of the contribution and compulsory contribution, either (a) by the parents or masters of those whose children attended, or (b) who had children of school age; or (c) by the inhabitants in general; or (d) by a combination of these methods.

2nd. That its language, likewise, gave sanction to the laying of a tuition-tax upon those who attended, or a rate upon every child of school age, or a town rate upon estates and " abilities," or any of them in combination, or any one or more in combination with any method or methods under the first head.

3rd. That income from land and endowment, and private bequests could be used in the support of the master as before. This source of income could be used in connection with any other method or combination of methods.

In brief, the law did not specifically alter any practice in the control and support of any town school. Each town had the same freedom in the choice of agencies and methods as before. How then were the practices modified? In the first place, the law made the school a civil institution. This was the cap-stone to a conception that had been gradually forming in those towns having town schools. The respect in which the General Court was held caused the full confirmation of this view. In those towns which had not established schools this point of view would have been taken in no uncertain manner. It was required by the highest civil organ in the colony; its establishment was im-posed upon the town and they were held for the enforcement of the act as a civil corporation. In the second place, while the law did not stipulate the town rate it implied the power to levy it. The conditions required it, and the result was practically the same as if it had been required.

These two general effects reinforced each other. The require-ment of a civil school carried with it the power to support it by the means of the civil tax. The use of the rate in turn furthered the democratic tendency in school control. As in the first period, so in this, it will be of advantage to treat first the

Methods of Raising the Master's Salary.

As the compulsory contribution had been an intermediate step in the evolution of the church rate and the poor rate in England, [1] so it proved to be in Massachusetts in the evolution of school support from the free contribution to one of the two forms of rate levied in support of schools. The development of the two divergent tendencies in the compulsory contribution have been noted; one, toward the regular town rate on estates and "abilities," the other toward tuition imposed and collected by authority of the town, called in this study, the tuition-tax. These two rates assumed definite form immediately after the passage of the law of 1647 and both continued through the century. This history we are now to review.

It will be of interest from two standpoints to break the whole period into two parts; the first embracing only the very first records in the different towns, and, the second, all the subsequent history. By this we shall see (1) that the abandonment of the compulsory contribution was immediate, in contrast to the persistence of the old tendencies of control; and (2) that the town rate was used more generally at this time than a few years later.

The different methods of raising the master's salary in 'use during the period were:

(1) The town rate.

(2) The tuition-tax.

(3) Tuition-tax on scholars attending and balance by town rate.

(4) Tuition-tax on all children of school age and balance by town rate.

(5) Town rate of fixed amount and all income from tuition-tax. (The last three are different combinations of the first two.)

The presentation of the records of the first few years may be made without further comment.

The first method was adopted by Charlestown in 1648. "It was agreed that a rate of fifteen pounds should be gathered of the town, towards the school for this year, and the five pounds that Major Sedgwick is to pay this year (for the island) for the school, also the town's part of Mistick wear for the school forever." In the margin are the words "allowance granted for a school."[2]   Newbury in 1652 and in 1653 levied a town rate:

---

(1) See pp. 20, 37 note.
(2) This record has been referred to previously as of doubtful date.   It is here given the date that seems most logical. (See page 36).   The reference made later to Charles-town in this chapter bears out this conclusion.

" Voted that there should be twenty pounds a year allowed for to maintain a schoolmaster out of the town rate." The record of the second year reads,— " At a general meeting of the town May 14, 1653 (?) there was ordered and voted that the town should by an equal proportion according to men's estates by way of rates pay four and twenty pounds by the year to maintain a free school to be kept at the meeting house and the master to teach all such inhabitants children as shall be sent to him so soon as they know their letters and begin to read." [1]

The plan of Dorchester in 1651 provided for support by the town rate and the method was followed up to and including 1653. This is evident from the following facts: In June, 1652, Mr. Butler, who was the master elected the previous May requested the selectmen " that the school rate may be gathered with the town rate." And it was listed with the town rate, " the rate for powder and the castle and the rate for the garrison debt," and undoubtedly on the same basis. The records of 1653 show a similar inclusion of the school rate in the list and also the item of the payment of the money to Mr. Butler.[2]

The record of the Boston town meeting in 1650 shows clearly the town rate: " It is also agreed that Mr. Woodmansey, the schoolmaster, shall have fifty pounds per annum for his teaching the scholars, and his proportion to be made up by rate." [3]

It is probable that the rate was the method of support first used in Watertown. In the record of the town meeting voting the contract with the master it is stated: " that the town did promise to allow the said Richard for his employment thirty pounds for this year." The selectmen later agreed with the master " that for his pay he is to have it, at two several times, the first at or upon the 29th of the 8th month (51) and the other pay upon the 12th of the 11th month (51)." [4] While these records do not establish this statement beyond a doubt, yet it is the most probable of all the methods.

The second method of support — that of tuition-tax — was adopted by Ipswich. In 1652, the school committee which was chosen " to receive all such sums of money, as have or shall be given toward the building or maintaining of a grammar school "

[1] Currier, Newbury, p. 395.
[2] Dorchester Recs. pp. 304, 306, 313, 315.
[3] Boston Recs. II. p. 99.
[4] Watertown Recs. I. p. 21.

were empowered among other things to " appoint " " from year to year what each scholar shall yearly or quarterly pay." [1]

It seems very probable that the Salem plan of 1644 developed into a tuition-tax system, with the tuition of the poor children paid by a town rate. This conclusion is based upon the town record of 1670, which stated that the master was to have 20 pounds from the town and " besides half-pay for all scholars of the town and whole pay from strangers." It seems from this that formerly the children of the town had given " whole pay," but that now in lieu of half of this the town would grant a rate.[2]

The only town adopting the fourth plan was Dedham. It was framed in 1652: " For the raising of the 20 pounds per annum for the schoolmaster's recompense, agreed upon the last general town meeting, it is ordered: (1) That all such inhabitants in our town as have male children or servants in their families betwixt the years 4 and 14 years of age shall pay for each such to the schoolmaster for the time being or to his use at his assignment in town in current payment the sum of 5 shillings per annum. (2) That whatsoever these sums shall fall short of the aforesaid sum of 20 pounds shall be raised by way of rating upon estates according to the usual manner. (3) That these sums shall be paid in two equal parts and proportions for the space of seven years next ensuing the first day of January, Anno. 1651 ; each half part to be paid at the end of each half year from time to time." [3]

The third and fifth methods were not adopted by any of the towns immediately after the passage of the law. They were the product of a later evolution.

The prominence of these two primary methods at this time is in line with the normal course of evolution from the compulsory contribution to the combined methods of the town rate and the tuition-tax. The town rate was the logical consequence of that tendency of the compulsory contribution which was, theoretically, imposed on all the inhabitants. For the strictly voluntary element in it, that in which each man stipulated the amount of his payment, must have become more and more unsatisfactory in its workings as the original spirit of the colony declined. As

[1] Felt, Ipswich, Essex & Hamilton, p. 83.
[2] Felt, Salem I. p. 432.
[3] Dedham Recs. III. p. 16.

this occurred, it then became necessary for the selectmen to fix the amounts which each should pay. Thus it approached closely to the town rate. When this stage was reached it became easy to adopt it alone. This had occurred in most of the towns previously in the support of the poor and in many of them in the support of the pastor.[1] The requirements of the law of 1647 forced its use in the case of schools also. In like manner, the tuition-tax was the logical consequence of that tendency of the contribution which caused only the parents and masters to pay toward the support of the master. Parents failed to give in just proportion and so the town was compelled to fix the rate. When the town was made responsible for the maintenance of a school, it was compelled in order to insure the support of the master to make the tuition a tax upon the parents.

The town rate and tuition-tax as single methods of support existed but for a short time in most of the towns. The town rate was combined with the tuition-tax in Watertown in the following year.[2] It existed alone in Dorchester for no longer than four years, and probably for only three:[3] In Newbury the town rate was levied for two years. The next record in schools, twenty-two years later, shows its abandonment.[4] The next reference to schools in Charlestown twenty years after 1647 or 1648 shows it to be no longer in use.[5] It is probable that it was dropped in these towns at an early date. In Boston it seems to have continued, but as will be shown later, custom had fixed an extra-legal payment to the master so that the school was not free of tuition charges to the pupil.

The abandonment of the town rate as a sole means of school support so soon after its adoption may be accounted for in this manner. The compulsory contribution from all the inhabitants left a large discretion to the selectmen. While theoretically each man was expected to pay according to his estate and his "abilities," the selectmen could easily not apply the rule rigidly to a wealthy man who had no or few children in the school. But when the town rate was adopted no such discretion was possible. It had to be levied on the same schedule as the

---

(1) See pp. 20, 37 note.
(2) Watertown Recs. I. pp. 21, 26.
(3) Dorchester Recs., pp. 304, 306, 313, 73, 82, 89, 96.
(4) Currier, Newbury, pp. 395-6.
(5) Frothingham, Charlestown, pp. 157, 177. The town records for these years are not now extant.

country or colonial, and town rates. This naturally aroused the opposition of the more wealthy inhabitants. On the other hand, the custom of tuition in the private schools was well known, and the previous application of the compulsory contribution had recognized the responsibility of the parent for the education of his child. Thus an adjustment was affected without great difficulty, which in effect carried on very much the same order as had existed under the voluntary contribution.

Tuition as the sole method of support persisted for a longer period. But as it was in all probability the custom for the town to pay the tuition of the poor children it was to some extent a combination of methods from the beginning. In Salem a town rate was levied in 1670, but soon abandoned because of the unusually large income from the school fund.[1] Of Ipswich we do not have data upon this point. Those towns imposing tuition alone would be led to adopt the town rate when tuition would no longer furnish a sufficient income for the school. And the fact that they already paid a rate as an item in the support of the poor would have made its further extension on the basis of the responsibility of society for the education of its children more easy.[2]

School support during the remainder of the period will now be presented. As has been indicated it is characterized by several plans which consisted of various combinations of the two primary methods, the town rate and tuition-rate. They were (3) [3] tuition-tax and balance of master's salary by town rate. (4) tuition-tax on all children of school age and balance by town rate. (5) town rate of fixed amount and all income from tuition-tax.

In but few towns was there uniformity of practice throughout the period. While most of them may be characterized on the whole as using one of these plans of support, yet the rule was variety of practice, and in some of them there was great variety. When one method was not working satisfactorily, they would

---

[1] Felt, Salem I. p. 432.
[2] It is of interest to note that this step completed the same evolution from voluntary support to a civil tax through which the support of the church passed. The lesser importance of the school combined with the fact that there was greater apparent disparity in the benefits received from it by different people permitted the partial abandonment of the plan.
[3] These numbers are those previously used at the beginning of this division of the chapter. See page 56.

try another. There is seemingly no general principle of evolution in all this change. It will be therefore best to treat each town separately under the plan which seemed to prevail either throughout the period or for the first part of the period as the conditions dictate.

A typical town of the first of those combinations and of the third method of support is Watertown. In January of 1652 Mr. Norcross was employed on the basis that [1] "every person that shall learn English only shall pay 3d. a week and such as write in Latin 4d.......and what the particulars do want of the full sum of 30 pounds the town doth hereby engage to make a supply." In the following December he was again employed "upon the same pay and the same privilege as he had last year."[2] In the years 1658 and 1659 are records of odd amounts due him which constitute the balance between the returns from tuition and his salary.[3] In 1660 "Mr. Norcross was chosen for schoolmaster for this year upon the same terms as in former years."[4] In 1662 the terms were stated "as in former times, with the addition of six pounds" Mr. Norcross was continued as master, and presumably according to the same arrangement, until 1667. This year tuition was abandoned and the town rate supported the school except for the tuition of children from outside the town. The record making this marked change of method reads:—"Agree with Mr. Norcross to keep school for the year ensuing for 30 pounds. And the town agreed that the school should be free to all the settled inhabitants; children that live in other towns to pay as before; and their payment to be deducted out of the 30 pounds; and the remainder to be made up by rate."[5]

The remaining part of the history of the master's support in Watertown may be most advantageously given in another connection. The fifth method was used for a considerable portion of the time. An association of individuals partially supported the school for a year or more also.[6]

Springfield after giving the master in 1677 an "encouragement" of land and what the pupils paid, agreed in 1678 to pay

[1] Watertown Recs. I. p. 26.
[2] Ibid I. p. 31.
[3] Ibid I. pp. 55, 58.
[4] Ibid I. p. 64.
[5] Ibid I. p. 91.
[6] See pp. 157-63.

him a stipulated sum, the "parents and masters of such as send their children or servants, being to allow to ye town according to their manner of allowance to the schoolmaster the year past." The town made up the balance. The same method was followed in 1683. In 1685 there was this modification. Instead of the scholars only paying, it was "agreed that all parents or holders be enjoined to send their children and servants, and that all persons from the Round Hill to the Mill River that do not send their children that are above five years and under nine years, that said persons pay for such children for the space of half a year after the rate of two pence a week." No record of method of payment occurs again for over 20 years. In 1706, it is provided that the "charge" of the school be carried on "according as the law directs." In the following year the scholars were assessed at the rate of three pence per week and the balance due the master was levied on the "town poles and estates." The law referred to was undoubtedly the colonial law of 1692, and the method was the same in both years.[1]

Dorchester followed the same method from 1655, when the selectmen took charge of the school. This conclusion is based (1) upon payment of money from the town rate in 1656 and thereafter, though insufficient to fully pay the salary; (2) upon insufficient levy in the town rate of 1657 for his maintenance; and (3) upon the following record of 1659 which provides for the rate upon scholars,— "At a meeting of the selectmen — there was a warrant given William Trescott (constable) for to gather of those parents and masters that sent their children or servants to the free school those sums that are in his list." In previous years the sums were paid without duress, or the empowering of the constable to collect was not recorded, or the town had not taken legal steps to enforce the payment — either of these three conditions might have held in these previous years which, from all outward appearances at least, seem to include a uniform policy of control and support.[2]

Northampton adopted this plan for one year in 1687.[3] Plymouth in 1698, and probably for several years thereafter, alternated between it and the town rate.[4]

---

[1] Burt, Springfield II. pp. 131, 137, 163, 173, 372, 373.
[2] Dorchester Recs. pp. 73, 82, 89, 96.
[3] Trumbull, Northampton I. p. 386.
[4] Plymouth Recs. pp. 270, 303, 316.

The fourth plan of school support—tuition-tax on all children of school age and balance by town rate—adopted by Dedham at the time of the transition, was not practiced in any other town for any long period of time. The plan of 1652 was a tax on all the children in the town and a town rate for the balance. In 1660 in levying the rate the order was,—" The school rate for the raising of 25 pounds and 5 pounds whereof is to pay Bro. Metcalf 12.10.3 being by town vote to be borne by the scholars, the other paid by estates at 1d. per pound." That all the children of school age were implied in the term " scholars " is proven by the selectmen's acts upon the same. Jonathan Fairbank, Sr., " made it appear that his youth is above age to pay the school rate, and it is therefore abated 4s. 9d. Ralph Day is abated 2s. because his son went out of town." In 1664 the rate was " at 3s. 6d. each scholar the number of scholars being 45," thus showing that the amount of the rate depended upon the number of children. The rate upon each in 1665 was 3s. 4 1-2d. In 1667 the record reads.—" A rate which is due from the male children that are capable to pay according to town order being assessed at 3s. 6d." The record of the school rate being imposed one-half on the children of the town and one half on estates is continuous to 1672. After this year there is no record of school support to 1679. Then the selectmen make a list of " names of such persons as are to pay to the school for their children." The record of 1680 is substantially the same, but contains only thirty names. We might be led to think that a new plan in which only the pupils of the school were taxed had been instituted were it not for the record of the year 1683 which tends to prove that the method adopted in 1660 still prevailed. " A rate made to defray town charges at 1d. per pound as deputy charges, etc., as also the one half the school rate; and the remainder of the school rate is raised upon the children as herein inserted." The small number of parents and masters included in the lists indicates strongly on the other hand that all the parents were not taxed by the selectmen, either in accordance with the expressed will of the town or of their own volition. Upon these points it is seemingly impossible to come to a decision. Possibly the legal method was that of 1660, and it was not practiced. We do know, however, that there was dissatisfaction with

5

the system of the master's support for in Jan. of 1685 a committee was appointed to consider the question.

The report of this committee was adopted. It provided (1) " that the one half of the school charges as well for quality as quantity shall be raised upon the rateable estates of our inhabitants whether nearer the school or further off. (2) That all such persons as dwell within one mile and a quarter from the school having male children shall pay for each child five shillings a year from six years old to twelve years old." It then fixed a less rate for those living between one and one-fourth and two miles, while those beyond this limit were freed from a rate entirely. Besides, there was a fixed rate for the grammar scholars. In the light of these acts of the town it would seem probable that the selectmen had followed a different principle in the levying of the rate than that laid down in 1660. This plan was the result of a demand of the outer sections, the same in character which in some towns produced the moving school.[1] This method was probably continued up to and including 1693, at which time there was considerable opposition to it. In 1694 the rate was imposed in the same manner as in 1660, at 1/2d. per pound and " every male above seven and under 12 at 3s. per head." In the latter part of this year and thereafter the rate was levied only upon poles and estates.[2]

The fifth method wherein the town rate was fixed at a certain sum and the remainder of the master's salary was left indefinite and dependent upon the number of scholars who attended was noted in the previous section as prevailing in Salem in 1670. It was continued up to 1677 when it was voted " that Mr. David Epps is called to be a grammar school master, so long as he shall continue and perform ye said plan in ye town, provided he may have what shall be allowed him, not by a town-rate, but in some other suitable way." This put support back upon the basis which existed before 1670 — income from land and endowment, and tuition. There was not another town rate for support of schools until 1734. Endowments here were comparatively many and returns from land were good. The tuition rate was fixed by town authority from year to year, according to the number of scholars and the amount of income from these sources.[3]

[1] See Chapter 10.
[2] Dedham Recs. III. p. 16; IV. pp. 16, 18, 91, 104, 140, 160, 199, 211; V. pp. 92, 98, 137, 159, 164, 222-3, 224, 229.
[3] Salem, pp. 432, 434-447.

Newbury in 1676 increased its "encouragement" to a substantial wage of 20 pounds and ordered that in addition the master should have what the committee and the master "shall agree upon for children that shall come to school to him." In 1678 and 1680 this method was evidently continued as the 20 pounds was voted each year. In '81 because of the interference of the General Court in fixing the amount of the master's salary at 60 pounds, the town was compelled to depart from its custom and to levy "a rate on the town in part, and the rest on the scholars that have been instructed by the said Mr. Emerson." In the latter part of the year they return to the old method by levying a rate of 20 pounds "for the payment of Mr. Bailey." The schedule of the scholars' payment is not given. Mr. Bailey's successor was paid "twenty pounds in good county pay, besides what the scholars shall give." This was the record of 1687. The town's vote on his employment stated "ye scholars to pay as formerly." Undoubtedly the method was continuous. In 1690, the master's salary was "25 pounds in town's pay — and the pay of the scholars according to custom." In the following year the master's salary was 30 pounds from the town, on condition he would teach "readers free, Latin scholars six-pence per week, writers and cypherers four pence per week." In other words the elementary school was free from tuition charges. This difference in payment of scholars was carried out in 1696, except here the distinction was between "the Latin scholars" and those "that come to him to read, write and cipher," the latter being freed from charges.[1]

Northampton followed this same plan — the fifth — from the beginning of its school in 1664 to 1671. In the first year the town was "to give Mr. Cornish six pounds toward the school and to take the benefit of the scholars." In 1667 the master was "to have out of the town stock ten pounds" and "four pence per week from such as are in the primer and other English books" and "six pence per week to learn accidence, writing, casting accounts." In 1671 it seems probable that they changed to the third plan though this is not positively affirmed until the year 1687.[2]

---

[1] Currier, Newbury, pp. 397, 398, 399, 400, 401.
[2] Trumbull, Northampton, pp. 141, 191, 193, 222, 383.

While these three methods of support were dominant during the period, yet there were two towns in which the town rate was the prominent method. These were Boston and Braintree. Yet there were in both towns certain additional charges. In the former town custom alone seems to have required it of the pupils. In Boston in 1683 at the time of the establishment of the two writing schools it was ordered that the master should receive twenty-five pounds from the town and " that such persons as send their children to school (as are able) should pay something to ye master for his better encouragement in his work." In 1741, the selectmen reported to the town that they did not find " any demand of entrance money made of the inhabitants." For " firing " however the master required of each pupil five shillings a piece. This " perquisite " as well as fees from out-of-town-children the master insisted on as " his right." These references establish clearly the custom of a charge upon pupils during this period.[1]

In Braintree, the records from 1678 to 1700 [2] mention only the town rate in addition to the support from the land. This may have been all; but the required payment of " quarter money " — a fee payable four times a year to the master — in 1668 [3] and probably in 1678, and in 1700 and 1703 [4] and probably to 1715, indicates a strong probability of its continuance in the meantime, as in Boston. The relations between the two towns were very close, many people owning property in both towns. They were, furthermore, the only two towns which contain reference to a payment to the master at entrance. These considerations strengthen this point of view. It is a matter however which cannot be settled.[5]

The master's support during the latter half of the seventeenth century was, on the whole, the period of a combination of the town rate and tuition-tax. Each of these elements was an evolution of one of the two tendencies in the application of the compulsory contribution in the preceding period. They were combined in three different ways, and the towns changed from one combination to another at will. Usually, in each town, one of them

---

[1] Boston Recs. II. p. 99; VII. pp. 57, 161; XII. p. 279.
[2] Braintree Recs. pp. 18, 20, 21, 27, 28, 29, 33, 39.
[3] Ibid, p. 9.
[4] Ibid, pp. 47, 54.
[5] It is well to note in this connection that Watertown used the town rate alone from 1667 to about 1690. Watertown Recs. I. p. 91—II. p. 39, passim. See pp. 167-8.

was the most prominent. Nevertheless, the town rate and tuition were the chief sources of support in addition to school funds in a few towns. These were, however, the commercial towns, and so had but little part in the creation of the moving school. The rural town [1] in which the town rate was prominent at one time abandoned it before the end of the century.

---

(1) **Watertown.**

CHAPTER IV

CONTROL AND SUPPORT OF THE CIVIL SCHOOL

PART II — AGENCIES OF CONTROL

1647-1700

The account of school control in those towns which had schools previous to 1647 is one of increasing democratization and secularization. Towns which established schools for the first time in response to the law or which did not increase to the size of fifty householders until a later time were generally democratic in the control of their schools from the first. The towns must therefore be divided into two classes.

Some new agencies of school control must now be reckoned with — the greater prominence of the temporary school committee, and the interference of the General Court in prescribing duties for the selectmen in connection with schools. Consideration of these processes may be postponed until after the movement in each of the towns is traced. The increasing democratic tendency in social and political affairs in the local centers requires attention, however, at this point.[1] The first generation was passing away with the opening of the second half-century. The generations which followed did not possess the personality, the ideals and the abilities of their fathers. The social bonds were loosened and the social ranks began to undergo a levelling process. This contributed to the independence of the individual in all of his interests and decreased the influence of the Elders in the settlements. The settlement by groups of people closely bound together by religious ties had come to an end, and the centers in the old towns had begun to extend outward in response to the economic interests of individuals.[2] The power of the Church had begun visibly to wane, so that by 1662 it was compelled to open its doors more widely, for fear that all distinctions

---

[1] Osgood, *Pol. Science Quarterly* VI. pp. 26-28. Here is an excellent brief summary of the developing democratic tendency in colonial affairs during the earlier period.
[2] See Chapter 6.

between it and the world would be obliterated.[1]   In response
to these changing social and economic conditions the qualifications for local citizenship were placed on a purely civil basis
in 1658.[2]   Then also, as town and colonial government developed, the functions and powers of the different officials became
more clearly defined.   There thus resulted a definite limitation
of the authority of selectmen in the control of schools.

It will be recalled that the powers granted the selectmen in
the earlier period were entirely or almost entirely unlimited.[3]
Dedham may be taken as an example.   In 1639 the selectmen's
powers were, " that whatsoever powers all ye whole company of
townsmen themselves so met together had......the very same
power is now given unto the selectmen.[4]   By 1651 this full
power had become limited in three particulars."   "(1) The admitting of men to the privilege of being townsmen.   (2) The
granting of a general dividend.   (3) The granting of farms.
In 1660 it was ordered that " a special committee be appointed
" to give instruction to the present selectmen."   This shows a
close supervision over their administration and the necessity of
a more careful limitation of their power than that which could
be given in town meeting directly.   That the town meeting itself
did carefully review their acts under these limited powers is seen
in the record of the general town meeting of 1671, which in all
probability indicated a custom.   The record of this meeting opens
with this statement: " The acts of the selectmen for the year
last past being read;" and then follows the record of the other
business transacted.[5]   The Boston records indicate a similar
tendency beginning with the year 1651.   The powers of the
selectmen had not been acted upon in town meeting for some
years.   At the annual meeting of this year after the election of
the selectmen a committee was appointed " to draw up the power
to be given the selectmen, which is first to be presented to the
town and consented to if they see cause."   In 1653, instructions
" in addition to what instructions they already have " were
ordered prepared.   In 1659 it was ordered that the " instructions
already given to the selectmen in writing be still in force till
the town presents others to them."   In 1660 this action was

---

[1] See Chapter 5.
[2] Mass. Col. Recs. IV., pt. I. pp. 335-6.
[3] See p. 37.
[4] Dedham Recs. III. p. 62.
[5] Ibid III. p. 5.   Ibid IV. p. 30.   Ibid IV. p. 197.

repeated.[1]   Unfortunately we do not have these instructions at hand.   It is safe to conclude, nevertheless, that the selectmen were now compelled to act within their powers as defined by the town meeting, and probably in considerable detail.   The day of granting of general powers had passed.

There were two types of school control in the towns during the latter half of the century,—the first, wherein the selectmen performed legislative functions; the second, in which the town exercised the legislative powers in town meeting.   The former was a survival of the old order previous to 1647, and was confined entirely to those towns which had schools at that time.   The latter was the new democratic tendency in school control.   The history of school control in the towns in the first class reveals a diminution in the powers of the selectmen, which resulted in a transition from the dominance of this agency in legislation previous to 1647 to full control by the town meeting before the close of the century.

Boston offers the clearest illustration of the movement.   In response to the law of 1647, which fixed the status of the school as a civil institution, full legislative action was taken by the town meeting in the year 1650 for the first time in the history of the town.   Strange to say, however, like action was not again taken for over thirty years, so that this record stands out isolated and appears to be almost an anomaly.[2]   The selectmen besides caring for the school property, school land, and the school funds, which would properly be included under their ministerial functions, did exercise full legislative power concerning the schools proper.   The recorded instances are as follows: (1) At a meet-

---

[1] Boston Recs. II. pp. 103, 114, 150, 154. The records of the other towns do not offer material for the study of this movement to so good an advantage. The writer sees no reason, however, for there being any difference between the towns in this respect. Obviously the subject belongs to another study which unfortunately has not as yet been made.

Chase in his History of Haverhill gives the following as the substance of the "powers of selectmen" voted by the town meeting (about 1670):

"They had power: 1. To order and appoint when Mr. Ward's salary should be paid, levy rates for the same, and to take them by distress, if not paid otherwise. 2. To observe all orders of the town, and collect all fines. 3. To pay all debts of the town, by fines due, or, by rates in general. 4. To make all rates necessary to defray the town's debts. 5. To call town meetings at discretion. 6. To see that all laws of the County were observed and kept. 7. To act in all prudential affairs of the town according to law. 8. To observe all orders of the town as near as they can."

This is the only record of detailed instruction that the author has met in his study. The contrast between them and those of the earlier time is evident. (Chase, Haverhill, p. 114.)

[2] The action was as follows:—"It is also agreed on that Mr. Woodmansey, the school-master shall have fifty pounds per annum for his teaching the scholars, and his proportion to be made up by rate." Boston Recs. II, 99.

ing of the selectmen in August, 1667, "Benjamin Thompson being made choice of the selectmen for to officiate in the place of the schoolmaster for one year, Mr. Hall [one of their number] being appointed to agree for terms." [1] (2) In 1670 Ezekiel Cheever was elected and installed in the following manner: " 22: 10: 1670. At a meeting of the honored Governor Richard Bellingham, Esq., Major General John Leverett, Ed. Tynge, Esq. Magistrate; Mr. John Mayo, Mr. John Oxenbridge, Mr. Thomas Thatcher, and Mr. James Allen, Elders; Capt. Thomas Lake, Capt. James Oliver, Mr. John Richards, and John Joyliffe, Selectmen of Boston. It was ordered and agreed that Mr. Ezekiel Chevers, Mr. Thomson, and Mr. Hinksman should be at the Governor's house that day sevennight to treat with them concerning the free school." At a meeting of the same men [2] held at the appointed time, " it was agreed and ordered that Mr. Ezekiel Cheevers should be called to and installed in the free school as head master thereof, which he being then present, accepted of, likewise that Mr. Thomson should be invited to an assistant to Mr. Cheevers in his work in the school, which Mr. Thomson being present, desired time to consider of and to give his answer ;— And upon the third of January, gave his answer to Major General Leverett in the negative,......" Upon the sixth of January 1671 these same men met and " repaired to the school and sent for Mr. Thomson who ......resigned up the possession of the school and school house to the Governor, etc., who delivered the key and possession of the school to Mr. Ezekiel Cheevers as the sole master thereof. And it was further agreed that the said Mr. Cheevers should be allowed sixty pounds per annum for his service in the school out of the town rates and rents that belong to the school, and the possession and use of the school house." [3]

(3) In the latter part of the year 1671, Capt. Daniel Hinksman, who had been usher under Mr. Thomson was " allowed £10 over and above his year's salary ending the first of March last as a gratuity from the town for not having sufficient warning to provide otherwise for himself." [4]

All of these acts are plainly legislative acts of a primary order. They were furthermore complete. To this point, except

[1] Boston Recs. VII. p. 38.
[2] There were seven selectmen at this time.
[3] Boston Recs. VII. p. 57.
[4] Ibid VII. p. 63.

for the act of 1650, there had been no change in the character of the acts performed by this agency. This practically unbroken series of similar acts proves conclusively the existence of this order of administration before 1647. However, this does not mean that the acts had the same sanction. The authority given to the selectmen before 1647 was general; here it was probably specific. The selectmen were probably delegated the power and assigned the duties involved in the complete control of the school by their instructions from the town meeting beginning about the year 1651.[1]

This complete control of the selectmen continued until 1689. In the meantime, however, the town passed upon three acts involving schools, all of which are in line with the prevailing tendency to place large powers in the selectmen. The acts of the town and selectmen during these years will now be reviewed.

The first two acts of the town after 1650 are to be joined together. They both relate to the education of the poor children. The first, that of 1679, simply referred to the selectmen a proposition which came up in town meeting regarding " a free school to teach the children of poor people." [2]   The burning of the almshouse in 1682 and the obligation of the town, because of an agreement with its donor to rebuild the same in such event, caused the second act. A tax was levied for the erection of a new almshouse and a committee appointed to attend to it. The amount of the tax was to be determined by the committee and selectmen acting in conjunction. Immediately after this business was completed " it was voted by ye inhabitants that the said committee with ye Selectmen consider of and provide one or more Free Schools for the teaching of children to write and cipher within this town." [3]

The first act of the selectmen during this period was taken in pursuance of the above directions. " It was voted by the said committee, first, that two schools shall be provided and agreed for: secondly, that the town shall allow £25 per annum for each school for the present; and that such persons as send their children to school (that are able) should pay something to ye master for his better encouragement in his work." [4]

---

[1] Co-operation of the colonial officers in 1670 was extra-legal. It is doubtless also a survival of aristocratic interference.
[2] Boston Recs. VII. p. 127.
[3] Ibid VII. pp. 157-8.
[4] Ibid VII. p. 161.

The second recorded act of the selectmen was in consequence of this one just given. Two of them " made return that according to a former order they had agreed with John Cole to keep a free school to teach ye children of the town to read and write for one year......for which the town is to pay him £10 in money and £20 in country pay as money, or at money price."[1] Here, again, are two instances of legislation of a primary order enacted by the selectmen. In connection with the record it is worth while to note that the provision of the first act regarding subjects to be taught and amount to be paid were not observed in the second. It is evident that the schools having once been established and the committee having ceased to exist by reason of the performance of the acts it was delegated to perform, the selectmen assumed the same unrestricted control as they did over the grammar school.

The third act of the town — 1685 — had to do with the income from land. It was of no consequence for it referred the question to the selectmen to whom it logically belonged.[2]

The next act of the town in 1689 — the fifth in its history — marks the turning point in the method of control of schools. It was then " voted that the former custom and practice in managing the affairs of the free schools be restored and continued.[3] The votes on this resolve tended undoubtedly to create a different regime of administration from that which had been prevailing. Their plans were plainly as indefinite as was their language. What they could have meant by the " former custom and practice " is almost beyond conjecture in the light of the evidence that no other order from even the earliest time ever existed unless it had been in the year 1650. Perhaps it was a knowledge of this record on the part of the supporters of the resolution that is responsible for the language used. When taking into account the fact that a radical change was evidently intended and that this was apparently to a more direct control of schools by the town meeting, this explanation of the wording of the act seems plausible. But whatever the interpretation of the act or the reason for the language used, the fact is that from this time on the people in town meeting did legislate more

[1] Boston Recs. VII. p. 171.
[2] Ibid VII. p. 174.
[3] Ibid VII. p. 197.

frequently and upon a greater variety of matters than in any previous period of the town's history.

To establish the fact that the town meeting did assume powers formerly delegated to and exercised by the selectmen, three acts of the town may be set off in contrast with three of the former acts of the selectmen.

(1) In 1690 Mr. Cole, who had been selected in 1684 by the selectmen for the reading and writing school, was elected by the town. The act reads:

" Ordered that Mr. John Cole be allowed to keep a free school for reading and writing and that ye selectmen agree with him for his salary.[1]

(2) In 1671 the selectmen had allowed Daniel Hinksman ten pounds in addition to his salary. In 1697 the town voted " that Mr. Cole master of the Free writing school of Boston shall have £10 added to his salary the year ensuing which will be £40 for said year." [2]

(3) In 1671 the selectmen first decided to have an assistant to Mr. Cheever, and since Mr. Thomson declined the place and Capt. Hinksman left, it is presumed they decided not to have any. Evidently they had full control of the decision of this question as well as of the salary to be paid.

In March of 1699, the town voted " that an assistant be provided with Mr. Cheevers in the Latin School. Voted further to be left to the selectmen, to make choice of the person, and to treat with him about his salary, making report thereof to the town." In the May following the selectmen had reported; for it was then " voted by said inhabitants that the selectmen shall agree with Mr. Ezekiel Lewis, for his salary as an Assistant to his grandfather Mr. Ezekiel Cheever in the Latin School, not exceeding £40 per year." [3]

These contrasted records need no comment to show the change in methods of control. It is to be noticed, however, that in the town's acts there is a progress with the passing of the years to a fuller assertion of control. In 1699 the selectmen act merely as a temporary committee for a specific purpose, and the amount of their direction is limited to a considerable degree.

(1) Boston Recs. VII. p. 200.
(2) Ibid VII. pp. 73,227.
(3) Ibid VII. pp. 57, 234, 236.

It does not seem necessary to cite other references to prove the fact that the town had assumed full legislative control and that the selectmen's duties had become purely ministerial in character. From this time the town retains direct control of its school affairs and the selectmen or the school committee are held constantly accountable for their acts.

School control in Dorchester during this period is characterized by an alternating policy in the relative powers of the town meeting and the selectmen. In the plan of control adopted in the year 1651,[1] the town exercised full legislative control, directed the selectmen to procure a master, and then ratified their choice and the contract, thereby levying the rate. This plan was followed until 1653. Then in general town meeting " it was voted that the selectmen should provide a school master for the town of Dorchester this present year." The selectmen hired the former master, but the agreement was not ratified by the town. The town two months later passed the rate for paying him.[2]

The selectmen in 1655 agreed with the master as follows: " It is agreed by and between the Selectmen of Dorchester for the time being on the one part in the behalf of the town and Thomas Wiswall and his son Ichabod Wiswall that Ichabod should teach " unto the end of three full years......all such children as by inhabitants shall be committed unto his care in English, Latin and Greek......and also instruct them in writing as he shall be able."......for which service " the Selectmen of Dorchester shall from year to year pay or cause to be paid unto Ichabod or his father by his assignment the full sum of twenty-five pounds two-thirds in wheat peas or barley merchantable and one-third in Indian....." In 1657 at a meeting of the selectmen " there was order given for the making of a rate of thirty pounds for the use of the school and town." At their meeting the following month " the selectmen did order that the constable should pay the school master £20 out of the rate abovesaid." At their June meeting in 1658 Major Atherton " was intreated to speak with the schoolmaster to know his mind whether he will keep school for longer time," and Mr. Potter was " intreated to look up what notes and papers he hath that concern the accounts of the scholars for the two years past, 56

---

[1] The town ended its system of aristocratic control by a board of feoffees in 1651. Dorchester Recs., p. 304.
[2] Ibid, pp. 313, 315.

and 57 ; and bring them to the selectmen." Both Atherton and Potter were selectmen.[1]

While it cannot be stated absolutely that the town did not perform a single legislative act, the weight of probability favors the conclusion that it performed but few. As has been shown in the second chapter,[2] absence of record favors action by the selectmen. Secondly, there is certain internal evidence in the records as given that points to the fact that the selectmen were taking the initiative in school affairs, which would strongly indicate that they performed some of the legislation, and probably a major portion of it. Had the town meeting exercised the legislative functions during these years we would expect to read, the *town* agrees to " pay or cause to be paid " the wages to the master and not the *selectmen*. We would expect also the town to pass upon the question whether it wished the school to continue instead of the selectmen inquiring of the master " whether he will keep school for a longer time."

In 1659 after the probable lack of a school during the previous year, at the general town meeting in March " it was concluded and voted that they would have a school kept in Dorchester as in former times." [3] Undoubtedly the selectmen passed the remaining necessary legislation. It is the continuation of the old regime and this record strengthens the point of view taken upon the character of the administration during the previous five years.

The following year events follow along a new course. The administration of the selectmen evidently was not satisfactory for the town took steps in rather a rude fashion. It ordered that " Mr. Poole is to keep the school until his year be ended. Also it was voted the same day that the selectmen are to labor to provide a schoolmaster by that time that Mr. Poole's year be ended." In 1661, 1664 and 1665 it was voted to have a school and Mr. Poole was elected in town meeting. Though the terms of his salary are not set forth, they were doubtless already fixed and the town meeting approved of them. In 1666 it was voted to have a school and a special committee of three was appointed " to endeavor to procure a school master " and furthermore it was agreed that " Mr. Poole should be spoken unto to go on in

---

[1] Dorchester Recs. pp. 73, 87, 89.
[2] See p. 49.
[3] Dorchester Recs. p. 97.

keeping school until another master be procured, at the same rate as formerly " and a committee of one appointed to see him. The committee failed and in 1668 the same action was taken regarding the continuance of Mr. Poole, and the same committee was instructed to perform the same office except at this time it was voted in addition, " they do give them full power to agree with such a man as they shall judge meet not exceeding forty pounds a year."[1]

Thus Mr. Poole, though his teaching seems to have been unsatisfactory, rendered a real service to the town of Dorchester in re-establishing direct control of the schools in the town meeting. Thenceforth the selectmen or the special committee acted under instruction of the town meeting and for limited periods. They now became solely the ministerial officers of the town. The amount of legislation performed by the town and the amount of authority delegated varied in different years. They usually employed the master, though in one year, he was elected in town meeting. This act involved the fixing of the amount of the money to be expended also. The manner of raising the master's salary seems not to have been altered from that followed in 1657-8.[2] Thus at the time when the printed records close, the town meeting was passing upon the most fundamental question of having a school; the selectmen were fixing the amount to be raised, though under supervision from the town, and the manner of raising the salary was established by custom.

Salem continued to leave the administration of her schools in the entire control of the selectmen. Finally in 1670, the town took its first action regarding schools after the passage of the law of 1647. At this time it assumed full control, instructing the selectmen to choose the master and to fix the amount of his salary. In 1677 the town elected the master and specified terms of agreement in a negative way. These included the fixing of the tuition, the details of which the selectmen arranged.[3] In 1699 the town in its written instruction to the selectmen said: " You shall give ye Grammar master such instructions and directions, as you shall think needful for regulation of ye school,"

---

[1] Dorchester Recs. pp. 102, 108, 121, 128, 136, 145.
[2] Ibid pp. 210, 182, 198, 228, 257, 268.
[3] Voted by ye town that Mr. Daniel Epps is called to be a grammar school master for ye town, so long as he shall continue and perform ye said place in ye town, provided he shall have what shall be annually allowed him, not by a town vote, but in some other suitable way. Felt, Salem, I. pp. 432, 434.

which covered, evidently, executive acts only. The selectmen, however, fixed the salary and determined for two succeeding masters how it should be raised, presumably under instructions from the town. In 1700 the inhabitants "without the bridge" were voted £15 annually for three years for the purpose of maintaining schools. In 1712 the school committee, which became a permanent institution, was first appointed. This was the beginning of a new regime in school control. Thus Salem, in general, is like Boston in its evolution of school control, though the details of it are not so clear.[1]

Charleston, and Ipswich[2] also, in all probability, belonged to this class, but the histories of the towns (there are no printed records) are not sufficiently full to permit the outlining of the process of development.[3]

In the second type of towns, the town meeting performed practically all the legislative functions and the selectmen acted as ministerial agents with very limited powers throughout the entire period. Watertown and Newbury furnish the best examples. Dedham is not strictly of either type. It is like the second in that its system of control was uniform and in that the selectmen acted under close supervision. It is like the first in that its selectmen were given considerable administrative discretion. It will therefore be given later as a system of control midway between the two general types.

There is no reference to a school in the records of Watertown until 1649. In that year the selectmen, probably acting under instruction from the town, directed John Sherman, one of their number, "to write a letter in the town's name unto David Mitchell of Stamfourth to certify to him the town's desire of him to come and keep a school in the town." Thirteen months later a different policy was pursued. The inhabitants in town meeting "voted and agreed upon that Mr. Rich. Norcross was chosen schoolmaster for the teaching of children to read and write and so much of Latin, according to an order of the Court, as also if any of this said town, have any maidens that have a

---

[1] Felt, Salem, pp. 430-9, 440, 442.
[2] Frothingham, Charleston, pp. 157, 177. Barnard's Amer. Jour. of Education XXVII. p. 127; XVI. p. 105.
[3] The records of Cambridge contain so little regarding school control that no adequate description of it can be given. It is very probable, however, that the selectmen administered the school—that is the reading and writing school. The grammar school was maintained as a private school with little action by the town. Cambridge Recs. pp. 293, 296.

desire to learn to write that the said Richard should attend them for the learning of them; as also that he teach such as desire to cast account, and that the town did promise to allow the said Richard for his employment thirty pounds for the year."[1]

This contract was passed in town meeting. It represents an extreme extension of legislative power, including as it does several features of acts that would ordinarily be performed by the executive organ of the local government. There was little left for the selectmen to decide upon, and their duties must have been little more than to see that the provisions of the town's act were met. Management of the school was as completely democratic as possible.

The unusual degree to which Watertown carried the minutia of administration into town meeting in 1651 was maintained quite consistently for many years. All of the four primary acts[2] of legislation were practically always passed in town meeting. In addition, the time for the beginning of the school, and the amount of firewood per pupil were likewise determined there. Only in one instance, in 1677, did the selectmen agree with the master, and then under express instruction from the town.[3] They did, however, in most of the years fix the time for the beginning of the school, the dates for the payment of fees, and decide upon similar questions of an executive nature. Nevertheless, it is seen that their discretionary power was of an inferior order and of a more limited extent than enjoyed by the selectmen of Dedham.

The people of Newbury acted less frequently through their town meeting than those of Watertown, but more frequently and in greater detail than those of Dedham. The town fixed the subjects to be taught in 1675 (the first year whose records are extant after 1653) in 1689, 1690 and 1691; fixed the wages and determined how they should be raised in 1677, 1680, 1687, 1689, 1690, 1691; and elected the master in 1678, 1681 and 1687. The selectmen acted entirely within the fixed limits of ministerial duties, which in character and number were midway between the two other towns.[4]

School administration in Braintree, Plymouth, Springfield and Northampton was of the same kind. The town meetings

---

[1] Watertown Recs. I. pp. 18, 21.
[2] See page 13.
[3] Watertown Recs. I. pp. 21, 110, 129. This statement does not apply to the time after 1680.
[4] Currier, Newbury, pp. 396-401.

passed practically all the legislation and even at times elected the master and passed the contracts, as in the case of Watertown. The selectmen's position seems to have been mid-way between that occupied by those in Dedham and those in Watertown with respect to the amount of their activity in legislation. Their duties were strictly ministerial in character and they were held to a close account of their acts.[1]   It is not necessary in this study to give a detailed description of this system.

The feoffees of Dedham in 1645 were given merely ministerial functions. This board came to an end with the act of 1651, which created a school for seven years, fixed the salary of the master and the manner in which it should be raised.[2   The law of 1647 was accepted as determining the kind of school. During this entire period the selectmen employed the master though there was no express direction to do so. It seems to have been accepted as one of the necessary ministerial acts. The powers of the selectmen and of the feoffees were thus the same. These thirteen years fixed the tendency; it was conformed to throughout with two slight variations. The town did not in every year or term of years signify its will to have a school. This was done in 1657, 1661 and 1662, and in 1676. The year of King Philip's war the matter was referred to the selectmen.[3]   The other years it seems to have been assumed. The other exception was in regard to the amount of the master's salary. When teachers became scarce, it was left to the selectmen to fix the amount. This was a proper extension of the ministerial function. The town elected the master in 1657, 1664,[4] the selectmen in most of the years thereafter.[5]   The town's acts were, in addition to the above, an appointment of a committee to represent the town in the receipt of a gift of money as an endowment for a Latin School in 1680, the appointment of a committee to propose a changed method of raising the master's salary, the adoption of their report in 1685, the abolition of the tax in 1694, and the " determination of the amount to be levied for support of school

---

(1) Braintree Recs. pp. 18, 20, 27, 33, 40, 47, 48, 50, 58, 70, 86, 75.
Burt, Springfield, I, pp. 131, 137, II, pp. 137, 163, 173 194, 368, 373, 380, 382
Trumbull, Northampton, I. pp. 141, 191, 193, 386, 426, 427.
Plymouth Recs. pp. 141, 224, 245.
(2) Dedham Recs. III. pp. 15, 16, 135, 193.
(3) Ibid III. p. 140; IV. pp. 27, 42; V. p. 40.
(4) Ibid III. pp. 140, 147, 149, IV. p. 83.
(5) Ibid IV. pp. 6, 32, 35. 67, 83, 133, 221; V. pp. 25, 41, 106, 125, 152, 209, 214.

in 1696.[1]   The administration was thus uniform throughout, the town acting only in an emergency, when a new condition arose in the path or when the old methods were becoming irksome.   The method of raising the master's salary was the same from 1651 to 1685.   The selectmen performed nothing outside of their proper ministerial duties except when specifically instructed by the town.   They never passed upon whether schools should be " kept " except when instructed, and they never determined the manner in which the salary should be raised; and their acts were reviewed at the annual town meeting as the first order of business.   Clearly the people were in control of their schools.

The permanent school committee, prominent in the period of the church town school, passed out of use within a few years after 1647.[2]   The only record of the existence of any in this period is furnished by Ipswich, where in 1652 nine men " were chosen a committee to receive all such sums of money as have or shall be given toward the building or maintaining of a grammar school and master."   They were given full power not only over the securing and disposing of the money, but also in the election of the master, the fixing of the tuition fees, and all matters concerning the incidental regulations of the schools.[3]   The length of time that this committee lasted cannot be stated positively. These facts show, however, the decline of the school committee modelled after the English board of feoffees.

The next step in the evolution of school control after that of control by the selectmen was control by the school committee as a strictly ministerial agency with definite powers.   During this period both the selectmen and the town occasionally appointed temporary special committees to execute their will in a certain matter, the committees of the town displacing for the time being the selectmen, and the committees of the selectmen performing their acts in the name of all.   The reason, presumably, for their appointment was the better or more economical execution of business.   The selectmen may have been overburdened or some of the inhabitants may have in a particular instance, because of certain personal or business qualities or relationships, been better qualified to attend to the matter

---

[1] Dedham Recs. V. pp. 98, 159, 164, 229, 240.
[2] Dorchester Recs., p. 304.   Dedham Recs. III. pp 15, 135.
[3] Felt, Ipswich, Essex, and Hamilton, p. 83.

in hand.   Manifestly there were many executive details within
the selectmen's affairs which required the attention of only one
or two men, and these they divided up among themselves and
reported back if necessary to the whole body.   At the time of
the establishment of the " moving " or " divided " school none of
the towns had established the school committee as a permanent
institution.[1]

Two laws passed by the General Court during this period require mention, as they affected indirectly the relative functions
of the town meeting and selectmen.

In 1654, the General Court passed legislation for the towns
in respect to the qualifications of those who taught in the schools
of the colony — in the College and in the town and private
schools.   By this act the overseers of the college and the selectmen of the towns were " commended " " not to admit or suffer
any such to be continued in office or place of teaching, education,
or instructing of youth or child in the college or schools that
have manifested themselves unsound in the faith or scandalous
in their lives, and not giving due satisfaction according to the
rules of Christ." [2]

This act is directed to the selectmen: and probably for three
reasons.   (1) They were as the ministerial officers of the town
or as its representative legislative body often entrusted with the
duty of securing the master of the town school.   (2) They
constituted a definite group of individuals who could be held
responsible by the colonial judiciary for the execution of the
law.   (3) It was their duty to look after the general interests
of the town and thus to inquire into the private schools.   But
the act did not from the standpoint of the evolution of school
control enlarge the functions of the selectmen, for they already
possessed the power of determining the qualifications of the master
in many towns from the beginning.   It defined certain qualifications which they must take into account in their exercise of
this power and thus constituted the beginning of state supervision of schools.   It did, moreover, affect the evolution of
control in one way — the selection of the teacher tended to remain in the hands of the selectmen as an administrative, rather
than as a legislative, function, but under the close supervision of

---

[1] See Suzzalo, Rise of Local School Supervision in Mass., pp. 59-67 for discussion of
development in detail.
[2] Mass. Col. Recs. IV. Pt. I. pp. 182-3.

the town meeting. Later it strengthened the tendency toward the creation of the school committee.

The law of 1692 while it held only the town as a corporate body responsible for the existence of schools and did not impose any specific duties upon the selectmen, yet they were required by the law to perform the acts prescribed for them by the town which they served. "And the selectmen and inhabitants of such towns, respectively [that is, towns of over fifty, and towns of over one hundred, families], shall take effectual care and make due provision for the settlement and maintenance of such schoolmaster and masters."[1] Doubtless the reason for the specific mention of the selectmen in the law was the failure of the selectmen of some of the towns to fulfill the duties expected of them by the town.[2]

The act, however, does not require of the selectmen that they should secure its enforcement, but rather that they should perform their functions as town officials, doing what they are instructed to do by the town. Thus the relation between town meeting and selectmen is not disturbed by the law except indirectly, as the mere mention of the selectmen may have induced some towns to recognize the selectmen in greater measure.

During this period the control of the school became firmly established in the people assembled in the town meeting. Control of a general and complete nature delegated to the selectmen or board of feoffees came to an end. The selectmen and special committees still performed administrative functions and a body of habits in this respect was developed in the different towns. It was the beginning of the formative period of American institutions. In respect to schools the people had had sufficient experience in direct control to enable them to frame definite practices. In the next century, out of this experience there evolved the American school committee with its own peculiar characteristics.

The period as a whole is to be characterized as one in which the people came to exercise direct control over their school in town meeting with a minimum of assistance from the selectmen. There was thus afforded a new basis for the creation of institutions.

[1] Province Laws I. p. 681.
[2] The failure of the selectmen of Dorchester to secure a successor to Mr. Poole in years previous may have caused the town to appoint a committee in 1666 and in 1668—Dorchester Recs. pp. 136, 145.

CHAPTER V

SOCIAL DISINTEGRATION

The first settlers upon Massachusetts soil were bound closely and firmly together in a brotherhood of common suffering and courageous undertaking for religious principles. Among them selfish interests were subordinated to the general good, the chief element of which was the perpetuation of a society in which the enjoyment of their religious life and the dominance of their creed to the exclusion of all others could be secured. It was these first settlers that possessed the charters and set up the colonial government; and they so fixed it that only those who could measure up to the religious qualifications could have any part in its administration.

Not all those who came over after the first voyage were Puritans, although they were Englishmen. These were treated as aliens. In consequence even as early as 1638 it was necessary to pass laws which compelled outward conformance to the Puritan regime. All those who remained conformed to the prevailing scheme of society though they did not contribute to the active promotion of it.

On the other hand, all, whether of their own number originally or of the alien portion of the population or of those seeking admission, who actively opposed the established institutions were persecuted even to the extent of banishment and death. They believed that only by these repressive and expulsive measures could the enjoyment and perpetuation of the true religious life be protected from the forces of the enemies that lurked on every side.

To preserve this unity of thought and action it was necessary that the inward life as well as the outward acts should be closely watched. The details of this feature of the Puritan civilization are too well known to receive anything more than mere mention here. As Doyle [1] suggests the colony was a " Puritan Sparta ruled by an oligarchy of believers trained by a pitiless system of spiritual and theoretical discipline." This custom of espionage

---

[1] Doyle, English Colonies in America, II p. 191.

of the private life established by the first settlers was imposed by them upon all who were at variance with their standards. By these measures of protection, external and internal, as complete a unity of purpose and of life as is possible in a civil society was preserved so long as the first settlers were in control. Those who were not in active promotion of the system were either in general sympathy with it or did not actively oppose it.

Religion being the chief object in the settlement, it not only became the strongest social tie that united the people into a social whole but it also practically excluded the literary and aesthetic interests. It absorbed the intellectual, dominated the political, and strongly affected the economic interests. The chief opportunity for social intercourse was in connection with the religious gatherings. The principal guide for conduct was the Bible. They were a people singularly devoted to religious ends, and every desire in life had to come under the purview of religious standards.

The active leaders of this unified society were the ministers of the churches. They and the leading men of the church worked in harmony. The latter filled the offices in the central government and to a large extent in the towns as well. Above these the ministry constituted a court of appeal to which those questions were referred which the civil officials did not feel competent to determine. The ministers and higher officials were men of great abilities. The fact that they had the hardihood and courage to carry out so unusual a scheme as that of the settlement, that they possessed the diplomacy to secure a charter which they could adapt to circumstances and to their own peculiar theories later, and the skill with which this adoption was effected — all mark them as being among the ablest men of their time. The followers were of various degrees of consequence down to the indented servant. They really affected the current of colonial life very little, while in local government they played a varying part.

An account of the weakening of the bonds which held the people together belongs to general history. Only the principal events will be here mentioned, and in a manner denoting the rate of progress and extent of movement rather than the forces which propelled it. Necessarily the account is one of the disruption of the church.

The Cambridge " Platform of Discipline " of 1648 expressed the highest realization of unity in the church state. A synod or council of churches could declare another church to be out of communion. Idolatry, blasphemy, and heresy either on the part of an individual or of a church were to be proceeded against by the civil government. " No sphere of church activity " was left " free from the possibility of interference by the civil power." This was approved by both local and civil government and by the church.[1]

The first division in religious affairs expressed itself in the passage of the " Half Way Covenant " by the Synod of 1662. Many of the children of the first generation and many of the emigrants not of the strict Puritan faith, though baptized in infancy, had not conformed to the requirements for membership in the church and declined to do so. Their children were growing up " excluded from the Baptism of Christianity and from the Ecclesiastical Inspection which is to accompany that baptism."[2] There grew up a party favoring the return to the old plan of admitting " all persons of regular life to full communion in the churches."[3] The demand for a modified relationship of some sort was too strong to be resisted. The Synod chose the half-way measure, which allowed " baptized persons of moral life and orthodox belief to belong to the church so far as to receive baptism for their children and all privileges but that of the Lord's Supper for themselves." [4] This solution was designed to prevent " the churches from so lowering the terms of full communion as to admit unworthy persons to all privilege." [5]

This act of the Synod indicates a loosening of the religious bonds — a weakening of the former rigor in preserving a unity of ideals and of life. In this movement most of the clergy participated, while its strongest opponents were found among the laymen of the first generation who were still living. It was a partial surrender to the enemy. And well might the ministry thus compromise, for even at this time a very large majority of the adult male population were not members of the church, and among them were some of strong ability and of undesirable in-

---

(1) Osgood, The American Colonies in the Seventeenth Century, I. pp. 214-5; Doyle, II. p. 73.
(2) Cotton Mather quoted by Dexter, Congregationalism, p 467.
(3) Ibid p. 469.
(4) Ibid p. 471.
(5) Ibid p. 472.

fluence in broad affairs.[1]   This new spirit of toleration is wit-
nessed also in the lessened severity in the persecution of the
Quakers and other sects, which reached its height just previous
to this time.   While it was destined to continue for some fifteen
years more, the change in the tide is to be noted here.[2]

Both of these events favored the development of individuality
and of diversity in the social ideals and practices. If the movement were permitted to continue, another basis for society than
that which was originally established would have to be con-
structed.   The first few years of the sixties mark the time when
the new tendency in the social life became sufficiently strong to
appear upon the surface.

From this time on the tendency grew apace. By 1670 the
effects of the movement were visible on every hand and were
thought by the faithful to be threatening the life of the colony.[3]
It was not only the dissensions that were growing up within
the colony that alarmed them, however.   In England, the Popish
king had again come into power and was threatening the security
of their rule.   Parties became differentiated on both political
and religious questions.   One party favored opposition to the
king on all questions, the other favored concessions in their
political rights so long as material prosperity was not endangered.
In the church controversy there were the parties of the Synodists
and Anti-Synodists, those who opposed and those who favored
the original church exclusiveness.   How far they were identical
it is not possible to determine.   It is sufficient to note, however,
that in each case there was the conservative and the moderate
party and that the unity of the old regime was rapidly passing.[4]

This division extended even to the ministry itself and from
this time on there is increasing divergence in the rules and
practices of the churches in the different towns.   Indeed, the
weight of the influence of the ministry as a whole favored the
liberal tendency.   This was most true of the pastors in the coast
settlements, where they were influenced by the leading men and
their business interests.[5]

On the other hand, while liberality of views on religious matters
gained wider currency and toleration in the churches increased,

---

[1] Osgood states that up to or by 1684, only about one in five of the adult male population were freemen.   The church membership could not have varied far from this. I. p. 212.
[2] Doyle II. p. 114.   Osgood I. pp. 285-7.
[3] Dexter, p. 475.
[4] Doyle II. pp. 191-4.
[5] Dexter, p. 474; Doyle, II. pp. 209-10.

the form of church government became even more oligarchical than before. The ministry were as eager for authority as ever and the declining interest of the people in religion and the church permitted them to gain increasing power. There was thus afforded the interesting contrast of increasing democracy in civil affairs and increasing oligarchy in church administration.[1] Again, it was a reflection of the change in the dominance of church and state which came about during the eighth decade, of the century.

Another division of the people is to be noted. The coast towns were the centre of the moderate party in politics and the liberal party in religion; while the inland towns were the homes of loyalty to the original form of colonial independence and of conservatism in upholding the old standards of religion, though they were weakening in regard to the standards of life.[2]

The events which mark the progress of the changing life should now be noticed briefly. In 1670 the church of Boston became divided over the Half-Way Covenant. Part of the church seceded and established a new church — the Old South. The right to secede was denied and the civil government took up the question after the Elders had decided it in the affirmative. The strength of the opposition was in the Lower House. A committee was appointed by it to inquire into " the prevailing evils which had brought God's displeasure upon the country," as an indirect method of censuring the seceders. Among the chief causes given by the committee was " declension from primitive foundation work and innovation in doctrine and worship," and the seceders were abused in caustic scriptural terms. But this action, which was alike in all respects to those of the early days, did not meet with the approval of even the inland towns, so great had been the change from the life and spirit of their forefathers. Over one-half of the Deputies were not returned, and one of the first acts of their successors was to reverse their proceedings in declaring that they knew " no just cause for those scandalizing reflections cast upon Elders, Ministers, and Churches." The right of secession from a church without its consent was thus established, and the domination of the church over the religious interests and lives of the people correspondingly

[1] Dexter, pp. 484-7.
[2] Doyle, II. p. 194.   Palfrey, III. pp. 359, 361, 368.

diminished. It was, likewise, a recognition of the growth of latitudinarian views and of the existence of two parties in the Church, each of equal importance. Finally, the second action of the Deputies reveals the great change of sentiment that came over the entire colony. They still stood for their church, but also for tolerance and the right of the individuals to withdraw from a church compact of their own volition and enter into another which expressed more liberal principles.[1] All of these worked to still further break up the unity and to promote diversity of beliefs, interests, and acts.

Doyle [2] fixes the above as the turning point in the political and ecclesiastical history of Massachusetts. The events of the decade that these acts ushered in, indicate the transition beyond a doubt. It was then that the persecution of the other sects came to an end. This may be illustrated in the case of the Baptists. In 1672 the law banishing them was reprinted. In 1679 a church was built in Boston and worship was begun therein. A law was soon passed taking it away from them, but the king intervened. The leading men of the church were afterwards called before the Court of Assistants but the only action taken was the nailing up of the house and the forbidding of the congregation to worship there longer. It was, however, opened by an unknown hand and worship was continued. The act of the General Court upon the matter when it came into session was to forgive the past but to forbid them meeting longer. The Baptists held services, however, in various parts of Massachusetts from that time on. This action was very mild as compared with that of twenty years previous.[3]

The passage of the Half-Way Covenant had caused a marked decay in the morals and manners of the people. They had met great calamities in war, on the sea, from the elements, fire, and pestilence, and these were interpreted as divine judgments. The synod of 1679 was called to consider this condition of affairs and to recommend a course for future action.[4] It is the conclusions of the synod that are of concern as throwing light upon the temperament of the ministry of that day. The points dwelt upon are moral and not doctrinal, their recommendations are

[1] Doyle, II. p. 193.
[2] Ibid II. p. 194.
[3] Backus, *A Hist. of N. E.* I, pp. 383–91 passim.
[4] Dexter, pp. 474. 478.

along the line of building up the character of men more than of strengthening the position of the church.   The church was to be used as an agency for the promotion of the best life of the individual but it was not conceived as being the dominant institution in the entire life of the people.[1]   The state instead of the church was dominant.   And the people found their unity in a still wider diversity and in a unity of a far different nature.

In 1684 the charter was annulled and the foundation of the support of the civil power in church affairs was cut from under the feet of the conservatives.   In 1684 the Episcopal form of worship was instituted in Boston, and maintained from this time on.   The influence of English officials and of English life in all its phases was a new source affecting the life and interests of all the people.[2]   This promoted breadth and divergence of views, and was hostile to the old traditions.   When in 1691 the new charter was secured, and from a Protestant king, the fears that had perplexed the staunch Puritan disappeared and they were content to recognize a still greater freedom in religious beliefs that were not Popish in character.[3]   The experience of the people with witchcraft taught them that they must think for themselves and not follow the lead of their pastors in religious thought and moral action as they were still somewhat inclined to do up to this time.[4]   This had its issue in the establishment of the Brattle Street Church through the leadership of William Brattle.   He and his followers were the first who " deviating from the established standard of the Congregational Church government, yet succeeded in getting themselves recognized as an orthodox body."[5]   By this time — 1700 — dissensions in the churches were not unusual and were often bitter.[6]   At the same time in many churches the requirements for membership were much relaxed.   Public confession of sins had long passed out of use and the private statement to the pastor was all that was ever required.   Men of lax morals were admitted in some instances if they desired baptism for their children, and those in " half-way " relations were admitted to the highest sacrament. In some towns the Lord's Supper was proclaimed as a means of

---

[1] Dexter, pp. 476-80.   Doyle II. pp. 209-10.
[2] Tiffany, C.—A Hist. of the Prot. Epis. Ch. in U. S., pp. 97-105 passim.
[3] Palfrey IV. p. 502.
[4] Adams, Emancipation of Mass. p. 236.
[5] Doyle II. p. 305.
[6] Ibid p. 377.   Trumbull, Northampton II. p. 200

regeneration and all men were urged to come to it. Members were admitted in wholesale fashion and with scant inquiry, statement, and ceremony. All useful distinctions between the church and the world were effaced. Add to this a more liberal and a less enthusiastic ministry who had come to have even a larger domination over the church as a whole, and the extent of its great fall from its previous high estate is seen. It was no more the dominant unifying force in society.[1]

The subordination of the church to the state — and a state in which the freeman and churchmembers were not identical, was fully effected at this time by the establishment of the province in 1692. From this time on the church was without the aid of its old powerful subordinate. While the ministry was supported by town tax as before, it was because a majority of the people willed it so — not because the church wished it. The unifying force had thus been altered. No longer was it possible to secure the calling of a synod or to get the government to aid in enforcing a stricter ecclesiastical discipline. The church was compelled to rely upon its own resources alone. And its members from the influence of the past years were constantly becoming more independent in their thinking and in their assertion of control in church affairs. The writings of Wise, which stood for democratic Congregationalism, appeared during the early part of the century. They reflected the best thought along this line, and increased the growth of the freedom of thought, and thus promoted diversity in belief and religious tolerance. " Social autonomy " rather than " congregational consolidation " became the characteristic of the churches.[2]

It was not long before other divergences in creed between the different Congregational churches was followed by the establishment of churches of other denominations. This movement was promoted by the provisional laws. By the law of 1692 [3] each town was compelled to support an orthodox pastor who was elected by the church and approved by the town. In 1727 the Episcopalians were allowed to pay their assessments to their own clergymen and in the following year the same privilege was extended to the Quakers and Baptists.[4] At this time, to estab-

---

[1] Dexter, pp. 474-5; 481-2.
[2] Doyle II. p. 378.   Walker, Hist. of Congregationalism in U. S., 209-10.
[3] Province Laws I. p. 162.
[4] Walker, p. 232.   Province Laws II. p. 494.

lish another Congregational church, the consent of the town was necessary. This was impossible to obtain in many instances, while to found a Baptist church no consent was required. Hence many Baptist churches were founded because of differences arising within Congregational churches either upon doctrinal or administrative grounds.

All of these acts promoted democratic opinion and institutions, and the greatest variety of views. They contributed to the prominence of the individual and to the fullest exercise of his own selfish interests. The bonds holding society together were no longer any form of religious belief or ecclesiastical despotism. The old order had passed away completely.

In its stead had come the purely civil society which existed for the promotion of the good of the individuals composing it, and not for the sake of the promotion of a peculiar life represented in a single institution. The individual had gained freedom of action in both private and public spheres. He was now at liberty to determine his actions within that broad limit of non-injury to others as fixed by laws, which he himself had a part in framing. This gradually increasing liberty had come in response to new interests and new wants, material, intellectual, social, and, on the whole, selfish. He was now ruled by commercial and wordly considerations as he saw them from his own point of view. Religion still had some hold on him, but not ecclesiasticism. This was subordinated to his own independent thinking. The regulation of society was the process of harmonization of all these diverse interests and tendencies so as to conserve the greatest good of all. The character of that process now demands our slight attention.

Without the mastery of an all-inclusive ideal or object in society which bound all together and determined the plan of the individual life and the conduct of the state, there resulted in this augmented and widened democracy a divergence of interests which were intense and deeply rooted in the minds and hearts of their possessors. Dissensions and quarrels, bitter and prolonged were inevitable.[1]   Each strove for all he could get. This

---

[1] In Northampton there was a division of the people into two parties known as the "court" and "country" parties composed of the chief men, those with wealth and authority in church and town, and those with less power, wealth and influence, respectively. (Trumbull's Northampton II. 36.) Framingham's population was divided into eight groups in which blood relationship, former dwelling places, and topography figured as factors. (Temple, in Hist. of Middlesex Co. p. 440.) Dedham had bitter contests over town officers for several years in the early part of the eighteenth century. These examples are given as samples outside of quarrels regarding church affairs which were more numerous

opposition promoted appeal to a careful endeavor to obtain exact justice for all. There was thus developed a keen sense of discrimination as to the rights of others, especially when those deciding the questions were disinterested, and a willingness to grant all that justice demanded. There were, however, many instances in which, behind the outward conformance with the legal decision, deep-seated animosities slumbered ready to break out again upon the slightest provocation.

This disruption of unity was universal. Opposition existed between neighbors, between sections of the same town, between different towns, between different parts of the colony. Colonial unity was not a well formed conception. The inland towns were not in sympathy with the coast towns; threatened danger to the shipping interests received only very slow response from them. Eastern and Western Massachusetts were separated as the Atlantic and Pacific states of the United States are today. In the towns each part wished equal benefits of the advantages afforded by the common funds. In a meagre settlement a division of these small returns would have nullified them to a large degree; dissensions were inevitable. Jealousy among individuals on account of honors conferred, as in the seating of the church, or regarding privileges of common land, or any other benefit of the town, could not be avoided. Society was in a condition of extreme disintegration which extended to all phases of life, public and private; disintegration in governmental institutions was the logical result. This, applied to administration of schools, brought about the moving school.

CHAPTER VI

DISPERSION OF POPULATION

The General Court after the first few years maintained a close supervision over the settling of the inhabitants. Title to all the land within the borders of the colony existed primarily in it and land could be occupied only by virtue of specific grants to individuals or groups of individuals. Grants of both kinds were made, though the latter were in the great majority. The Court went further in the regulation of settlements, however, than the issuing of title to land; it fixed the manner in which the land should be distributed among the individuals in the group, and in doing this and other things it did not hesitate to interfere in the affairs of any town in any respect whenever it deemed fit.[1]

The form of settlement required was that which was assumed voluntarily in the earliest settlements. The land was held in common proprietorship by those to whom it was granted and by those who were admitted to equal rights by the original grantees or their successors. It was distributed among them according to the will of the majority. But in this distribution it was necessary that the house lots be separated from the tillage and pasture land, and be grouped together in compact fashion. Beyond this central core lay the farming and grazing land, held in common or individual proprietorship. The core contained the church and, when there was one, the school house as well. It was located usually on a stream the valley of which offered the most fertile of the poor land which the colony afforded. Outside the appropriated land of each settlement lay the untamed forest wilderness. The desire for land was great and the amounts granted to these quasi-corporations was almost always far above the amount that could be utilized. As a result the towns were separated from each other by broad bands of forests, through which only faint paths ran, connecting the settlements.

This compact form of settlement was chosen and insisted upon for various reasons. Their fear of the savages, doubtless, was a compelling reason in the first few years. Then, too, their com-

---

(1) Osgood I. pp. 429-34.

mon privation and sufferings, and the strong demand for co-operation in the building of the houses and the providing of food and clothing, also promoted it. Finally, the large part that religion played in their lives made close settlements desirable by the church members, and the maintenance of their established form and character of society required it. The law which gave expression to their convictions along this line was passed in September 1635 and amended the following year. According to this no " dwelling house " should " be built above one-half mile from the meeting house " in any town in the colony.[1]

While it is certain that this half-mile limit was not closely observed in all the towns (for these acts were repealed as early as 1640) [2] yet it is equally true that the " village mark " did prevail in all of them, but with slightly extended borders. In 1639 the General Court ordered that the weekly lecture in its churches should close sufficiently early to permit those who lived a " mile or two off " to get home by daylight.[3] This rule was intended most probably, however, to benefit the people of only a few towns — those most scattered. The laws enforcing attendance at church worship were of such a nature as to make dwelling near to the church very desirable[4] and this operated upon the individual settler. The town corporation as the owner of the land was during the first decades enthusiastically ortho-dox and, doubtless, it took care of the recalcitrant members who wished to settle beyond the pale. An instance of this which is, probably, quite typical of many not recorded, is fur-nished in Ipswich in 1661. Here a man's land was sold by the " seven men " because the distance of his home from the meeting house had caused him to absent himself from its services, " in order that living nearer the meeting house he might more con-veniently attend public worship," and this act was approved or directed by the General Court.[5]

It was in this compact form of settlement that the church-town school spent its entire existence, and in which the civil school had its birth as well. But with the changing social order and the alterations in ideals which accompanied it, combined with

[1] Mass. Recs. I. pp. 157. 181.
[2] Ibid I. p. 291.   Watertown Rec.s, I. p. 4.   Doyle II. p. 14.
[3] Felt, Eccle. Hist. I. p. 387.
[4] Mass. Recs. II. p. 118.
[5] Hist. of Essex Co., p. 204.

7

changes in external conditions, the core was dispersed and the dwelling houses were located upon the outlying farm lands. The reasons for this and the progress and extent of the movement must now be considered briefly.

All of the forces which caused close settlement at the beginning were losing their strength. The edge of their emotion consequent upon the character of their undertaking was being dulled by the experiences of time. Religious fervor was dampened by the many difficulties encountered in gaining subsistence. Their unity of life was weakening to the extent that the individual interests were receiving additional consideration in the determination of affairs. And the fear of the Indian was lessening with intimate acquaintance. Added to these modifications in the attitude of the original colonists, which, although comparatively slight at first, grew from year to year and generation to generation, was the increase in population.

The influence of this latter factor working with those above was to cause the granting to individuals of more and more of the unappropriated farming and grazing land. These later grants were at a greater distance from the centre necessarily, and thus the weight of the argument of convenience of dwelling house to farm received increased support. This process was carried on until all the land had been taken up in the original town which, under the limitations imposed by the town as to residence, could be worked with a fair return. When this point was reached, the establishment of new settlements came to be considered and additional factors entered into the problem.

These new factors were the quality of the land just beyond the limit of appropriated land as compared with the land in the other prospective centers, and the ties of family, kindred, and friendship. If at the time of the maturing of the new generations the quality of the land was poor, then the question resolved itself into whether these ties should be broken by the departure of one, or whether they should be maintained by the one remaining to his disadvantage or by the departure of all. If the quality of the land was good in the new centres, these personal and selfish considerations struggled with the declining spirit of the old regime until they triumphed.

But the establishment of new centres involved other considerations than the mere quality of its land. The distance from market, from friends and relatives, and the dangers of the wilderness and from Indians were all of weight. Also, there was a limit set in various stages of Massachusetts history to the frontier settlements. Finally, the General Court took care in the granting of its land that the interests of the colony as a whole as well as of the petitioners for the new grant should be secured. It canvassed the situation thoroughly and passed upon the questions of the grant with reference to the effect of their act both upon the old and upon the prospective settlements.

All of these elements taken together as determined by the individuals, town, and the General Court, influenced the spread of the population. Up to the second decade of the eighteenth century it can be differentiated into two general stages, the first closing with about the year 1660 and marked by the restricted settlement and the dominance of the interests of the group, the second, beginning at about that date, characterized by a gradual dispersion of the settlements and the dominance of individual and economic interests.

The passage and repeal of the law fixing the limit of dwelling house at one-half mile from the meeting house and the laws compelling attendance at church worship have already been noticed. Also, the drastic action taken by the towns and the courts have been illustrated by a typical act. By these the first period is clearly characterized. Those conditions which fix the close of this period at about this time are:

(1) The ceasing of efforts to penetrate further into the wilderness in the establishment of new centers. The towns on the outermost limits of population in 1650 in the eastern counties of Massachusetts Bay Colony were Salisbury, Haverhill, Andover, Chelmsford, Groton, Marlboro, Concord, Sudbury, and Medfield. In 1679 the towns named as frontier towns by the General Court were substantially the same.[1] Salisbury was omitted because Exeter was north of her; Groton because it had been destroyed; none were added. The list in 1700, besides the isolated settlements of Mendon and Lancaster and the towns on the Connecticut river, contained substantially the same towns as these and none farther removed from the coast.[2] The increase in the population must have been provided for, therefore, either by an

---

[1] Mass. Col. Recs. V. p. 79.
[2] Prov. Recs. I. p. 402.

extension from the centre of the limit of dwelling houses and of farms in the towns already settled or by a removal of the people to new towns along or within the borders of the frontier. These latter were, evidently, less desirable tracts and so the tendency to expand within the town intensified.[1]

(2) The number of towns settled diminished considerably. Taking the territory of the original Massachusetts colony, the settlement of new towns began to fall off as early as 1650, but with a still greater decline after 1660. This decline continued until 1710 when there was a very great increase in the number of towns founded. Up to 1650 thirty towns had been founded, an average of seven and a half to each period of five years. During the first and second half of the sixth decade there were two and five respectively. In the succeeding five year periods to 1680 there were three, one, five, four. Two of these four were settled before the opening of King Philip's war. After 1679 the numbers for each five year period to 1710 were two, none, three, none, one, one. To be sure, this was likewise the period during which there was the least increase of population, but up to 1675 the natural increase must have been considerable, for early marriages and large families were universal, though in fact mortality was high; and the children when they reached the age of twenty or thereabouts had to be provided with farms. The small number of new towns founded between 1660 and the breaking out of the war — a total of eleven — is not sufficient to provide for the normal increase of a population which contained possibly thirty thousand in 1660 and fifty thousand in 1700,[2] provided the manner of settlement remained the same. For these nine towns did not at a liberal estimate contain more than an average of forty householders. The increase in population must have caused therefore an extension in the radius of settlement in the older towns.

(3) The social reconstruction which was just coming to the surface at this time in the passage of the Half-Way Covenant, in the diminution in the severity of the punishment of Quakers, in the rising democracy, undoubtedly affected the minds of all and

---

[1] This failure to push farther out at this time shows in itself a diminution in the religious-social ardor that had characterized the original settlers. Had it been preserved unaffected by selfish economic interests, the line of settlement would have pushed out gradually and uniformly, each town being of that extent that would have afforded the proper condition for the cultivation of the religious life.

[2] Adams, *Three Episodes of M. Hist.* II. p. 671.   Doyle II. p. 386.   Palfrey IV. pp. 135-6.

made it easier for the farmer to follow more and more his own selfish interests. The towns would at least be less averse to fixing a limit and of enforcing penalties against its infraction, if such existed. The General Court took no action directly. Its laws against non-church attendance must have received, in the changing spirit of the community, more laxity in their administration.

(4) The year 1661 marks also the last effort on the part of an organized body as a church or town to establish a new settlement. The earlier mode of settlement was most frequently by congregations, or large parts of congregations. Towns had taken the initiative in this matter as well,— Salem in 1639 and in 1643, [1] Salisbury in 1645, [2] Cambridge regulated its village at Lexington until 1640. [3] Initiative from individuals, either in large groups or small, was the rule thereafter until 1661, when Dedham attempted to establish a village on its own land at a point which later became Wrentham. [4] The old group-congregational bond of union seemed no longer to be effective. The interests of the individual were paramount. Eight men and their families went of their own accord and twelve years later there was a sufficient number for them to have a form of local government for themselves. But the settlement was built up by a process of slow accretion.

These four considerations indicate the abandonment of the old idea concerning methods of settlement and the dominance of the interests of the individual causing scattered settlements.

While up to about 1660 the size of a community seems to have been largely influenced by considerations of the religious welfare of the group, after that date this became of minor importance, and the settlements took into large account the welfare of the individuals composing them. Undoubtedly, this gradual expansion of the old towns and the settlement of the new would have progressed steadily had it not been for King Philip's War and the French and Indian Wars, which followed after them in the last decade of the seventeenth and the first decade of the eighteenth centuries. The effect of these wars was to drive in the inhabitants from some of the frontier towns and to check the

(1) Hist. of Essex Co. I. p. 414.
(2) Ibid p. 411.
(3) Hist. of Middlesex Co. II. p. 13.
(4) Worthington, Dedham, p. 23.

impulse in the more courageous to penetrate the wilderness in quest of better lands. Sad to relate, five or six thousand of young men were killed in battle, many of whom would probably have become the head of a large family, and thus the normal increase in population was prevented.[1]

Upon the form of settlement these wars had two opposite effects, according to whether the town was exposed to danger or whether it was secure. Because of the increased danger the people were inclined to take up farms of poorer quality in the least exposed towns, thus expanding the circumference of settlement. Towns on the border were compelled by the General Court, in language which suggests the liberty that men had previously been taking in determining their place of settlement, to restrict their settlements to closer bounds. This act provided " that no deserted town or new plantation shall be inhabited until the people first make application to the Governor and Council." The form of settlement was to be fixed by a committee appointed for the purpose and in the planning of it " they are required to have a principal respect to nearness and convenience of habitation for uniting against enemies, and more comfort for Christian communion and enjoyment of God's worship, and education of children in schools, and civility with other good ends."[2]

Some of the towns in the interior still endeavored to limit the distance of the dwelling houses. Thus Dedham in 1682 placed the limit at two miles.[3] But this does not seem to have been successful for by the end of the century the original village was occupied but by a few farmers and the farm houses were scattered widely over the town.

The town records, the church records, and the colonial records bear repeated and continual reference to the spread of population within the town. New congregations were organized within the towns, and the proper civil government for administering them

---

[1] Hutchinson II. p. 183.
[2] Mass. Col. Recs. V. p. 214.   The border towns even to 1725 were compelled· as a means of protection to keep their dwelling houses near each other.   Many of these towns probably did not maintain schools regularly, however.   And so long as they remained compact they were in the same period of development respecting schools as the original settlements.   When the dangers from Indians were removed they spread out rapidly and the school soon followed.   From the standpoint of development of schools this class of towns were in the small minority. Trumbull, Northampton II. pp. 38, 15-32, 98, Weeden, Soc. and Ec. Hist. I. 271; Worcester Recs. II. 9-39.
[3] Worthington, Dedham, p. 15. Mervin, Dedham, p. 55.

established. This subject will be more fully treated in Chapter eight, to which the reader is referred.

It remains here to discuss the form which this expansion took. There was no uniformity. The course followed depended first upon the natural advantages offered, and second upon the vast complexity of motives in the individuals who desired more lands. When the land was divided by lot another set of factors entered in to influence the location of the dwelling houses of the different settlers. Quality of soil, accessibility to the village, nearness to neighbors or to other members of the family, were all prominent factors in the process. The irregular distribution of the better land and the topography of the country often caused the settlements to extend radially within narrow limits and in a few main directions from the centre. In some towns a new and smaller village was formed in a distant part of the town. While in some instances the form of settlement was compact and roughly circular in type, yet in others it is to be compared more to a nerve centre with its accompanying nerves.

Thus the same town presented an appearance in the early eighteenth century far different from that in the middle seventeenth century. At the earlier time, it was an oasis in a forest desert which was difficult to penetrate; at the later time, although much of the land was still untilled, yet comparatively little of it in the older settlements was unused. The concentrated population about the single church had dispersed until it was scattered over much of the town's territory. Smaller sub-groups of population were forming within the different towns, set off to themselves by a range of hills, by a stream, or by mere distance from the centre. These were developing their own common interests and in many cases a second church was erected within the town. Likewise in administration of civil affairs districts were erected for greater economy and convenience.[1]

The influence of this changed method of settlement upon the creation of the moving school is apparent. It made it more difficult for the head of the household to attend town meetings several times a year, and for the family to go to public worship on Sunday, but many times more difficult upon the days intervening for the children to go to the town school in the centre.

---

[1] See Chapter VIII.

Hence this factor produced a necessity for a new adaptation of means to end.

The difficulty—the practical impossibility of children traveling far to school is appreciated more fully, however, when the severity of the winters, the spring floods, the extent of forests, the poor character of the woods, and the barriers presented by the swamps, fords, lakes, streams and high hills are pointed out.[1]

For the first points mere mention will suffice. The hardships endured by the colonists in the winter season are well known to all; the spring floods did not differ from the floods of today. The amount of land covered and the duration of the floods may be judged from the fact that at the present time in Essex County one acre out of every two hundred and seven is " fresh water meadow covered by water in spring," and for that reason is exempted from taxation by the state.[2]   Originally, the entire land was covered with forests excepting along those streams which afforded meadow. It was upon these streams that the centre of the settlement was usually placed, near a spring upon a sandy spot which was unfit for cultivation.[3]   The amount of forest varied in different towns, but in many the dwelling houses outside the centre were placed in the midst of forests. It was because of this that the Indians were able to steal upon a household without being detected. This occurred several times about the beginning of the century. Wolves and wild cats infested the country. The greatest number of wolves was killed in the last years of the seventeenth century — about three hundred per year in the entire state, and after that time about one hundred per year to 1738. Two thousand two hundred wild cats were killed within seven years in the second quarter of the century. Besides these, bears and catamounts were occasionally seen and shot.[4]

Water furnished the chief means of communication at first, and roads in the town led to the stream upon which the settlement was made or to the ocean. In 1639 the General Court ordered highways to be laid out connecting all towns along the

---

[1] These same facts show the necessity for extension of settlements radially and its impossibility by concentric circles.
[2] Sears, Geology of Essex County, p. 394.
[3] Ibid p. 23.
[4] Judd. Hist. of Hadley, p. 352.   Hanson, Hist. of Danvers, p. 38.

coast.[1] Towns themselves took the initiative in laying out roads to adjoining towns with which there was some common interest, commercial or otherwise. By 1700 these main thoroughfares had become fairly well established although travel by coaches had not yet begun.[2] Within the towns themselves roads to the centre from the principal groups of settlements, and likewise to the mill had succeeded paths connecting farm to farm.[3] Aside from these main roads other ways were probably in most cases undefined and ofttimes on private land. If marked out, they shared the fate which often befell the most prominent road, of being ungraded and almost uncared for. Travel at its best was upon horseback, though horses were rather scarce and not well bred. For the pedestrian and rider nothing more than the bridle path was needed. For heavy articles the best means of transportation was the heavy ox-cart. As there was comparatively little carrying of goods to market at that time, there was not a demand for good roads. A stump or a stone was not an impediment, and the width of the road, often ten rods, permitted the finding of a path through the trees or around a muddy place. They were not laid according to any system. Sometimes the court complained " they are felt too straight and in other places travelers are forced to go far about." Ferries and bridges over some of the larger streams on the principal roads were common, but the smaller streams in the case of less important roads had as yet to be forded. It was not an unusual thing for the road between two places to be nearly twice as long as it is today.[4]

But these difficulties are not appreciated until a thorough study is made of the topography of the country. Not until then is it seen that of necessity the population must have been scattered and communication difficult. The wonder is that the people were able to cope successfully with the situation. Essex County is taken as an example. In topographical features it is typical of all of the territory at that time settled in Eastern Massachusetts. This county is irregular in outline but in general conforms to a square with its sides at an angle of 45° with the lines connecting the main points of the compass. Its territory exclusive of the

---

[1] Mass. Col. Recs. I. p. 280.
[2] Weedon. pp. 113, 311, 409, 509, 510.
[3] Currier, Newbury, p. 415. Judd, Hadley, p. 375.
[4] Torrey, Fitchburg, p. 42. Mass. Col. Recs. I. p. 280. Marvin, Lancaster, pp. 65-70; Trumbull's Northampton I. p. 165.

tidal rivers and bays is equivalent to that of fifteen congressional townships. Thus it corresponds roughly in size to many western counties four townships square. Carrying out the analogy, its sixteen thousand five hundred acres of peat swamps, which vary in depth from six to fifteen feet,[1] if evenly distributed, would make for each township an area of one thousand one hundred acres or one and three-quarter sections out of thirty-six in an entire township. In fact the swamp land is distributed quite generally over the entire county and, with the exception of the great Wenham swamp, in a fairly even manner. In size and shape there is the greatest variety. Many of them are long and narrow, others wide and broad. In addition to these swamps there are many lakes and fords. Sears in his *Geology of Essex County* [2] says that there are eighty which are worthy of notice and then gives a list of sixty varying in size from three to four hundred acres (three estimated). The size of the median lake is forty-two acres and there are a sufficient number clustered about this point in the distribution to permit us to call it a modal point as well, although there are ten of them of either eighteen or twenty acres and five which cover sixty acres. The limits of the second and third quartiles of the distribution are twenty acres and sixty acres. Were the total lake surface evenly divided between the fifteen townships, each would have two hundred and seventy-eight acres covered with lake or pond water — almost a half section. If the number of lakes were evenly distributed, each township would have five or six. Besides these two geographical features taking up land which might otherwise be cultivated, and badly interfering with communication between the different parts of the country, is another which operates in both these points only partially. The fresh-water meadows, if distributed evenly among the fifteen townships, would make one thousand one hundred acres, or one and three-fourths sections for each. These three features taken together would make for each township a total of two thousand four hundred and seventy-eight acres or three and seven-eighths sections—almost one-ninth of the territory. In addition, setting up a barrier to communication at every point met, are seven " extended " streams.[3] Emptying into them or into the ocean are, also, twelve smaller " consequent " streams, along

[1] Sears, p. 394.
[2] Pp. 400-2.
[3] Ibid. pp. 394, 27-34.

some of which are the fresh water meadows. One of the former, the Merrimac, runs along one side of the irregular square and forms a basin in the northwest part of the county. The other streams take their origin from a point south of this and in the north part of the county and flow toward the ocean to the east and southeast. There is thus formed a close network of streams over the whole county.

The last natural feature affecting the course of settlement was the hills. Along the seacoast as far north as Essex there is a range of hills that are quite close together, steep though not high. Another range in the northwest part constitutes the watershed. Besides these there are one hundred and ninety-three drumlins and nineteen bedrock hills scattered over the county. These stand out, in general, singly, rising in many instances abruptly to a distance varying from forty to three hundred feet above the level of the surrounding country, the distribution of the middle quartiles lying between one hundred and one hundred and sixty feet.[1] Their bases vary in shape from that of an elongated ellipse to a circle. The distance along the longest diameter varies from one-half to one and one-half miles, and along the shortest from one-quarter to three-quarter miles.[2] The median diameters are probably close to five-eighths miles and three-eighths miles respectively. They are distributed quite evenly over that part of the country north of the range of hills along the southern seacoast except in the south part of the present town of Boxford, which is near the centre of the county. This territory approximates in size twelve congressional townships. Thus there are on the average seventeen hills to each township and one to almost every two square miles.

Careful thought upon the above statements will enable the reader to construct in imagination a topographical map of the county. The frequency and even distribution of streams and hills over the entire county, of lakes over all except the peninsula of old Newbury, and of swamps over all except the Merrimac region, and the manner in which all are intermingled is striking. The country as a whole is low, the highest point being only four hundred feet above sea level and this on a hill which is two hundred feet above the general level of the surrounding country.

(1) Sears, pp. 395-8.
(2) Ibid, Geological Map.

The topographical map presents a picture of hills set here and there, usually singly, although there are several ranges and groups, upon a low level country, and interlaced with small and large streams, lakes, and swamps. There is not a point in the country more than three miles away from a river or lake or swamp, and, excepting the territory in modern Salisbury and ancient Newbury, there is not a point two miles distant from one of these hindrances to communication; and, frequently, two or three of them, and even all, are within this limit. The plain in Newberry, which is triangular in form having a base and altitude of six miles each, and the rectangular plain in Boxford four by two and one-half miles, are the largest surfaces presenting no obstruction to travel.

Thus the peculiar topography of the country scattered the population, increased the distance because of necessary detours, and multiplied the hindrances to easy communication between the different parts of the towns. The pressing demands of earning a livelihood from the infertile soil prevented attempts at over-coming the difficulties. The climate and the dangers of the wilderness added their shares to the grievous task of going from place to place.

The conclusion is patent, that after the land was well settled the central school was very difficult and often impossible of access during part of the year. For those in the distant sections to share equally in the privileges of the town school with those in the centre, it was necessary that it be placed in the outlying parts of the town.

CHAPTER VII

INTELLECTUAL DECLINE

The same struggle between religious and economic interests, which by the triumph of the latter produced social disintegration and dispersion of population, caused also a marked alteration in educational ideals.

Early Puritanism demanded for the welfare of the individual and for the perpetuation of the church-state high intellectual standards; on the other hand, the hard struggles to gain a livelihood and the accumulation of the comforts of life required at its best but a small portion of the learning given in the schools. Therefore, as religion became increasingly formal and as the state gained the mastery over the church, the people failed to respond to the former sanctions for educating their children and were governed more by economic considerations; consequently, there was a decided lowering in the amount and quality of instruction given. This decline, was due also, in part to the difficulties encountered by a pioneer people, and to the disturbed condition of affairs on account of the wars.

The moving school appears at the point when, educational interests having reached their lowest ebb, the people became conscious of the deplorable state of affairs and attempted to better their conditions.

This decline in the interest in education and its changing character need now to be traced. As a background, all that which has been stated in the previous two chapters concerning the decline in religion and morals, the parallel rise in economic motives, and the character of the difficulties which the environment offered to the colonists in the efforts towards its subjugation, must be kept in mind.

The laws of 1642 and 1647 were in response to a fear that education was not receiving proper consideration in the towns. The economic difficulties incident to the ceasing of immigration and the consequent fall of values and disruption of trade, coupled with the departure of some of the colonists and many of the ministry, were the chief causes of their passage.[1] The " Declaration concerning the Advancement of Learning " in 1652 reflects the fears of the leaders for the future in the point of a sufficient number of educated persons to continue the life of the colony as it was then constituted.[2] That all the towns did not obey the law as to maintenance of a school is evidenced by the fact that fines were imposed; [3] that others maintained the kind of school required by law in order to escape the fine and not because the inhabitants wanted that kind of a school is likewise evidenced in the language of the town records.[4] Thus it was difficult even during the first years of the civil school while the original purposes in the establishment of the colony still prevailed above all other considerations, and before the population had begun to disperse widely from the original village, for the people to maintain schools of the standard thought necessary to sustain the prevailing order. This was due, undoubtedly, to the changing attitude of the people already manifested in religion and to the increasing weight of material arguments.

The decline from this time on is difficult to trace. In 1671 the General Court doubled the amount of the fine on towns for not maintaining a grammer school,[5] and in 1683 increased it to twenty pounds on towns of over two hundred householders.[6] One of the evils which, according to the Act of the Synod of 1670, had brought God's disfavor upon them was " a lamentable lack of public spirit, causing schools of learning and other such common interests to languish, and raising murmurs as to philanthropic expenditures."[7] The election sermons before the General Court in the year 1672 and for many years thereafter complain likewise of the want of schools.[8] These facts establish a general opposition to the maintenance of the grammar school, even though by this time its curriculum had become so modified that in the inland towns it was chiefly a reading and writing school.[9]

The low estate to which education had fallen in the last quarter of the century may be indicated by the school history of two

---

[1] Eggleston, Transit of Civilization, p. 229.   Weeden, I. pp. 165-6.
[2] Mass. Col. Recs. IV, Pt. I. pp. 100-1.
[3] Currier. Newbury, p. 396.
[4] Watertown Recs. p. 21.
[5] Mass. Col. Recs. IV. Pt. II. p. 486.
[6] Ibid V. p. 414.
[7] Dexter, Congregationalism p. 478.
[8] Felt, Ipswich, p. 433.
[9] See later paragraph.

towns whose printed records are complete for the period, and which represent fairly the condition which prevailed in probably a large majority of the inland towns.[1]

The records of Dedham and Watertown reveal entire absence of schools during some years, a school of shorter term than that required by law in some of the years when it was maintained, and lack of interest in education during the entire time. Dedham maintained a school of annual sessions continuously up to 1673. This year the records make no mention of the school, and, according to the town's historian, the town was fined the following year by the colonial court.[2] In 1674 the school was maintained for but one-quarter of the year. During part of the time between 1676 and 1678 there was probably no school, for the power to decide whether there should be a school was in 1676 delegated to the selectmen and there is no mention of a school until 1678. This interruption was due largely to the war, and for that reason seems to have been disregarded by the court. During the years 1685 to 1690 there seems to have been a failure to support a school for part of or all that time.[3] As a result the town was again fined in 1691.[4] Again in 1692 it seems quite probable there was no school, though there is no record of the imposition of a fine.[5] The school was kept but for one half the year in 1679, 1681, 1691, and 1701, for but one quarter in 1693, and for but two months in 1690.[6] The action of the town in 1685 in ordering the schoolmaster " to desist and leave off keeping school at the end of the present half year " not only indicates the lack of a school for a part of the time, but also probably a custom of having half-year sessions. For the same master had kept the school since 1681 when the session was for a half year and the intervening records do not tell the length of the terms.[7]

Watertown likewise maintained a continuous annual school up to 1686.[8] The records for the next few years indicate failure to provide for a school during a part of the term. The town then

---

[1] As to the extent of this indifference to education it is impossible to get absolute evidence. It must have been general however, as judged by the contemporaneous references, the acts of the courts, and the later low state of education among adults.
[2] Dedham Recs. IV. p. 221; V. p. 25; Worthington, Dedham, p. 55.
[3] Ibid V. pp. 25, 39, 103, 159-209, passim.
[4] Worthington's Dedham, p. 55.
[5] Dedham Recs. IV, pp. 214-22, passim.
[6] Ibid V. pp, 87, 106; 214, 287, 222, 209.
[7] Ibid V. pp. 159, 137, 153.
[8] Watertown Recs. II. pp. 26-39 passim.

in 1696 voted to " keep " a school " according to law." In 1696 the town sent a committee to the Court of Quarter Sessions " to pray the Court not to impose a fine on the town ; and to inform the Court it is hopeful that the town will be provided with a school before the next quarter session." The records indicate there was no school again in 1698 and, in consequence, in 1700 the town appointed a committee of four " to apply themselves to the quarter sessions to pray for the abatement of the fine that was set on the town for want of a school according to law."[1] Watertown, as Dedham, seems to have had a school for but part of the year at various times, in 1686 and 1704.[2] The judges of the Court seem in all these instances to have been lenient in not requiring the full letter of the law.

The town records of other towns fix the end of the school term at a specified time which was not a full year from the commencement of the school.[3] This seems likewise to have been satisfactory. And, indeed, it is not to be wondered at that in the condition of affairs the judges were lax or that the members of the grand jury failed to discover or report infractions of the law.

The lack of interest in schools is revealed in other ways than by reference to the customary time which the schools were maintained. Watertown, which since 1667 had been supporting its school wholly by the town rate, would not in 1690 do anything more than grant fifteen pounds toward a master's maintenance. A company of twenty persons then guaranteed a sum of ten pounds additional and the master was secured.[4] This shows general apathy among the many, and commendable interest among the few. Seven years later at a town meeting it was voted in spite of the law not to have a grammar school, but within a month, probably because of the presence of others in the second meeting, this action was rescinded.[5] The act reveals the temper of the people. As a whole they did not want schools and they would pay no more in the town rate than was absolutely necessary to escape the fine, for it was an expenditure of money with no return. They would oftentimes prefer to take their chances, hoping not to be reported to the Court, but in that event,

(1) Watertown Recs. II. pp. 108, 132.
(2) Ibid I. pp. 26, 152.
(3) Currier's Newbury, p. 396; Plymouth Recs. pp. 99, 246, 270.
(4) Watertown Recs. II. p 63.
(5) Ibid II. p. 110.

and also in case of the fine having been imposed, they would present every excuse that they could think of to escape the actual payment of the money.

The dishonorable artifices practiced by the people of Woburn to get around the difficulty presented by the provincial law is of interest in showing the opposition of the people to schools. In 1703-4 they employed a Mr. Bradstreet of Andover who came and was "personally at Woburn at the time of Charlestown court" to receive all children who came to him for instruction. But, as it happened, no children appeared, and he returned home. For this trip he received his expenses and "eighteen shillings in silver for a gratuity." This was a less amount than a fine, and the school committee deemed it was performing its best service to the town in planning a method by which the town could most easily avoid the expense of a school. This same method was used in later years in the same town, one man being paid "for standing in school master two courts." If the town was presented at these sessions, as it probably was, it could have been solemnly affirmed by the town fathers that they had contracted with a teacher, as was the case, that he was on the ground ready to receive all scholars who came to him, and that, therefore, the town was not liable to a fine. But they told not the whole truth and here was the dishonorable subterfuge, which does not appear to have pricked their consciences in the least. It is, indeed, a notable instance of indifference to the advantages of an education.[1]

But it does not follow that when schools were maintained throughout the year that the children of the towns were in constant attendance. But very few attended all the year, and most of them for but a few months.[2] That it was probable that but few scholars would attend the school in Watertown during the spring and summer of 1694 is indicated in the contract with the master. This provided that upon the first of April he was to begin teaching at the school house, and "then, if upon a month's trial at the school house there appeared not a considerable quantity of scholars then he has liberty to keep all the year at his own house."[3] In Braintree the established tuition fee was known as the "quarter money." That it was usual for scholars to.

---

[1] Sewall, Woburn, p. 214.
[2] Trumbull, Northampton II. p. 222.
[3] Watertown Recs. II. p. 62.

8

attend school but a quarter at a time in this town is shown by
the town's act in 1700. " Voted — every scholar shall pay for his
entry into the school one shilling and so successively for every
quarter for the whole year *if he shall go more than one quarter.*[1]
That some children in Boston did attend school but little, if
at all, is evidenced from the acts of the town in 1682 when it
built its almshouse and established two elementary schools. By
the latter act the same committee which was to build the almshouse was also to " consider of and provide one or more free
schools." The preamble to this act states that " many more
persons and families that misspend their time in idleness and
tippling with great neglect of their callings and suffer their children shamefully to spend their time in the streets."[2]   Two
schools were established and instruction in them in reading, writing, and ciphering was offered free of charge to all the children
of the town. Since these were the first two schools in Boston
to furnish elementary instruction and the only way in which this
had been previously afforded was in the family and in private
schools, it follows that the education of some was totally neglected.
That this was the case with some or even many families living
on the outskirts of some of the rural towns far away from the
central school is just as certain. The fact that these people were
brought before the selectmen and admonished for their neglect
is ample proof, and records of this character frequently appear.[3]
The acts of the Massachusetts General Court in restricting the
limit of population in the new and abandoned settlements implies
it, as does also the act of the Connecticut legislature of similar
purport, a few years later.

The decline in interest in the education of the old type is observed in the altered curriculum of the grammar school. The
subjects of instruction in the school at Dorchester as presented
in the " rules and regulations " of 1645 were " humane learning,
and good literature and likewise good manners," and the " principles of the Christian religion." In 1655 the subjects ordered
were English, Latin and Greek and " writing as he [the master]
shall be able." In 1676 Greek had been dropped out and writing was given an equal standing with Latin and English or

[1] Braintree Recs. p. 47.
[2] Boston Recs. VII. pp. 157-8.
[3] Watertown Recs. I. pp. 103, 107, 109.   These are good typical instances.

reading.[1]   This omission of Greek was general.   The general tendency in the rural towns was to give only as much Latin as would satisfy the legal requirement and to make of the grammar school as far as possible an elementary school.   This tendency appears early in Watertown, where in 1651 the master was to teach " to read and write and so much of Latin according to an order of the Court."   In Newbury in 1675, the master was to teach " to write and read and cipher and teach a grammar school." The chief interest was in the " necessary pieces or parts of learning videl: reading and writing " as it is stated in the acts of the inhabitants of Springfield.[2]

The time given previously to the classics was occupied partially by instruction in the elements of arithmetic.   This subject known as " casting accounts " or " ciphering " was added by the towns to the curriculum of the elementary school as specified in the act of 1647.   As interest in the languages lessened in those towns where grammar schools were required, arithmetic supplanted the languages as far as the courts would permit.   By 1700 most all towns having the elementary school only gave instruction in it in addition to reading and writing.   It seems on the whole to have been paired with writing, the pupil taking writing, pursuing also arithmetic.[3]

The social and economic conditions of the times in the rural towns did not demand an education.   The general pursuit was farming carried on under adverse conditions.   Learning to read the primer, psalter, and catechism brought no economic return, for they were not better prepared for their work after going to school than before.   Furthermore, to read and write did not open the way to further knowledge of their occupation.   Neither did it offer a means of knowledge of things happening throughout the world.   For there were practically no books other than the Bible except among the ministry; there were no newspapers, no post offices or post routes for letters.   Intelligence of the outside world came by word of mouth, and but infrequently and slowly. Moreover, the people were little interested in this intelligence except when their own liberties were endangered.   They were a

---

(1) Dorchester Records, pp. 56, 73, 198.
(2) Watertown Recs. p. 21. Currier, Newbury, p. 396. Burt, Springfield I. p. 137.
(3) Trumbull, Northampton II. pp. 193, 389; Frothingham, Charleston p. 177; Boston Recs. VII. pp. 158, 240; Plymouth Recs. pp. 141, 270; Watertown Recs. I. p. 21, II. p. 132; Cambridge Recs., p. 296; Currier, Newbury, pp. 396, 400; Felt, Salem, pp. 439, 440.

simple, plodding, industrious, unaggressive, honest race, knowing little and caring less for anything beyond their own restricted horizon. Education had gained its sanction from their fore-fathers largely on religious grounds. They venerated their deeds and perpetuated their institutions, but they had almost lost the spiritual quality which gave these institutions their life. The school remained and was regarded theoretically as a good thing. But the presumption of the good in it as formerly conceived was largely lacking. The old sanction was gone, and a new one had not as yet taken hold of the people with sufficient force to cause them to provide schools of their own initiative. Education, once guided skillfully and with a definite purpose and regarded as one of the most important concerns in the social life, was now neg-lected for the more selfish and immediate ends of a much more restricted social life.

But there was another prominent reason for diminution of interest in schools, political in character, though it produced pro-found economic effects. The hard times first felt in the forties were succeeded by years in which through strenuous effort the people were just beginning to establish themselves on a satis-factory economic basis when in 1675 the trouble with the Indians began.[1] After this until the time when the period of this study closes financial stringency and poverty had to be struggled with on account of the continuance of the difficulties with the savages and the political conflicts between England and France. Whereas in 1670 only one-half the country rate was levied and in 1670 none at all, in the ten years from 1675 to 1684 an average of five and one half rates were assessed upon the people. Within five years more increased taxation was again imposed on account of King William's War and continued through many years.[2] These wars, moreover, caused the temporary abandonment of some towns, and the serious interruption of the daily pursuits in many others. Every town, furthermore, was more or less affected, even if secure from attack, by the departure of the men as soldiers.

The political troubles thus brought on poverty which in some towns was sorely felt.[3] This economic result in turn seriously affected the problem of school support, both in the case of the town rate, for the people were already taxed very grievously,

[1] Palfrey III. p. 133.
[2] Collection of American Statistical Associations I. pp. 248-90.
[3] Hazen's Billerica, p. 69.

and also in the case of the tuition-tax on scholars. The payment of the latter being dependent upon attendance, many parents no doubt chose to keep their children at home rather than to pay the tax. This force, beginning to work in 1676, had by the close of the century promoted an indifference in which there was little or no appreciation of the benefits of an education.

The educational acquirements of the people at this time—about 1700—is reflected in the records kept by the town clerks. This office was regarded as very important and only those specially skilled in the art of writing and proficient in expression of thought and in spelling were chosen. These records show a low standard of ability to have been almost universal among the rural communities. Neither were the town officers skillful in keeping accounts in a systematic way. Many men and almost all women signed legal documents by their marks.[1] The general apathy which these facts reveal could not have promoted schools.

Though it is difficult and probably impossible to get at the exact extent of this general indifference to schools at the close of the seventeenth century, yet it seems plain that there was a visible tendency to dispense with the reading and writing school as well as the grammar school in some towns. The evidence to support this view is found in the facts, that the laws of 1692 and 1701 included the reading and writing school as well as the grammar school in the clause imposing a penalty for failure to obey the law, and in the statements of the law of 1701 covering the reasons for its enactment, while the laws of 1647, 1671, and 1683 provided for penalties upon the towns for non-maintenance of the grammar school alone.[2] This act of 1692 after re-enacting substantially the law of 1647 continues: " Every such schoolmaster to be suitably encouraged and paid by the inhabitants. And the selectmen and inhabitants of such towns, respectively, shall take effectual care and make due provision for the settlement and maintenance of such schoolmaster and masters. And if any town, qualified as before exprest shall neglect the due observance of this act, for the procuring and settling of any

(1) Of thirteen men conveying a piece of the proprietor's land to the town of Manchester in 1716 eight made their mark. *Records*, p. 133. Walcott, Concord, pp. 132-3; Sewall, Woburn, p. 54; Judd, Hadley, p. 64.
(2) Mass. Col. Recs. II. p. 203; IV. Pt. 2, p. 486; V. p. 414.

such schoolmaster as aforesaid, by the space of one year, every such defective town shall incur the penalty of ten pounds for every conviction of such neglect * * * " (1)

The law of 1701 (2) repeats in the preamble that portion of the law of 1692 which is the re-enactment of the law of 1647 and enacts " that the penalty or forfeiture for non-observance of the said law shall henceforth be twenty pounds per annum and so proportionately for a lesser time that any town shall be without such settled schoolmaster respectively."(3)

The statement of the law of 1701 which indicates the tendency to get along without the elementary school as well as the grammar school is in the preamble: " Whereas it is by law appointed — (then is inserted that part of the law of 1692 which specifies the kind of schools for each town) — the observance of which wholesome and necessary law is shamefully neglected by divers towns, and the penalty thereof not required." It would seem that if the towns which were required to have only the elementary school generally observed it, this law of 1701 would not have included them in its provisions. And the fact that the penalty for them is placed at a figure which was well nigh the amount of a master's salary indicates plainly that the failure to obey the law was more than an exceptional occurrence. Probably it was not so frequent as the failure to maintain the grammar school, but such an act was the more grievous and therefore deserved as great a penalty. All of these statements in the law may be taken to establish beyond a doubt that both the elementary and grammar schools were sadly neglected in many places.

While these laws reveal the extreme decadence in educational affairs, they likewise show the turning of the tide toward improvement. This is particularly true of the law of 1701. It expresses a stiffening tendency among the leaders of the state.

---

(1) Prov. Laws I. p. 62.
(2) Prov. Laws I. p. 470.
(3) It seems probable that the penalty of five pounds in the law of 1647 was intended to apply to the reading and writing school also though it is not so stated in the law. The increased fines in 1671 and 1683, however, applied to grammar schools alone. The decision of these points must wait until the records of the courts are printed, a work that is now being carried on for Essex County. Granting, however, that the fine of five pounds was assessed against towns for not having a reading and writing school up to 1691, the argument is not invalidated. The author has not met, however, with a fully substantiated instance of a town being fined for the failure to maintain a purely reading and writing school at any time during the entire period of the study, though it is evident that the towns hastened to get a schoolmaster as soon as the number of fifty householders were reached. It is difficult to get material upon this point from town records because the towns which were of the requisite size for a reading and writing school at this time either have not published their records, or they were so poorly kept that no reference is made to the fine.

Not only is the fine increased to an amount which would go a long way toward the payment of the master and the choice of the grammar school master guarded so as to insure a teacher of good ability, but in addition the custom of employing the minister of the town as master was expressly prohibited. The enforcement of the laws was also better secured by the following clause: " And the justice of peace in each respective county are hereby directed to take effectual care that the laws respecting schools and schoolmasters be duly observed and put in execution; and all grand jurors within their respective counties shall diligently inquire and make presentment of all breaches and neglect of the said laws, that so due prosecution may be made against the offenders."

The towns felt the force of this law and at once responded, often much against their will, by maintaining schools more regularly. In the case of Watertown, one of the two towns which were taken as typical of those towns not fully observing the law, [1] compliance with it was thereafter constant. The enactment of this law in consequence of this upward trend among those who had the destiny of the state in charge had much to do with the creation of the moving school. Its effect can be best shown however in another connection.[2]

It is worthy of note here that the school was regarded as an agent of social conservation on the new basis of the civil state. The school having lost its moorings was now well in hand again but under a new master — the state and not the church. The civil school of the church-state had become the civil school of the civil state. Its purposes were to prevent " the nourishing of ignorance and irreligion," [3] to propagate religion and good manners, and thereby serve as an agent against " intemperance, immorality and profaneness;"[4] and not to get " the true sense and meaning of the original " scriptures which otherwise " might be clouded by false glosses of saint seeming deceivers,"[5] nor " to fill places of most eminence as they are empty or wanting," (i.e. in state and church).[6] The masters were not therefore compelled to meet the qualifications that they had not " manifested

---

[1] Watertown Recs. II. p. 139.
[2] See Chapter X.
[3] Law of 1701, Prov. Laws I. p. 470.
[4] Laws of 1712; Prov. Laws I. p. 681.
[5] Law of 1647, Mass. Col. Recs. II. p. 247.
[6] Declaration of 1652, Mass. Col. Recs. IV. Pt. 1, pp. 100-1.

themselves unsound in the faith or scandalous in their lives,"
and could give "due satisfaction according to the rules of
Christ "[1] (i.e. as set forth in the established church); but
rather in the case of the reading and writing school masters
nothing was stipulated, and in the case of the grammar school
master only that he was to be "some discreet person of good
conversation, well instructed in the tongues."[2]   These intellectual and moral qualifications were to be passed upon after
1701 by the pastors as those most competent to determine
these points, but their power did not legally pass beyond them.[3]
The law of 1712,[4] which refers to private and not public schools,
carries out the same principle.   Religion is regarded as necessary to morality, but ecclesiastic domination of the individual and
the state is absent.   The school was provided by the state for
the purpose of giving every child the opportunity of gaining the
rudiments of an education, intellectual and moral and religious,
which would make him a good citizen without fixing arbitrarily
the mold into which he should conform.   The school, from the
point of view of the individual child on the other hand, was
regarded as giving him a means for his fullest and freest development without reference to any preconceived pattern into which
his personality must fit.   The school was thus for both the good
of the individual and of the state.   The state by securing the
best interests of the individuals composing it conserved its own
best interests; the individual thus obtaining the good furnished
by the state enriched himself and thereby the state.

With the recital of two incidents in local history, one of which
pictures alike the lowest point of interest and the beginning of
the upward tendency as well, and the other, the new relationship
of the school to the community as just presented, this chapter
will close.   The first incident occurred in Danvers during the
last years of the first decade in the eighteenth century.[5]   This
locality was then known as the "Village" of the town of Salem

---

[1] Law of 1654—Mass. Col. Recs. IV; pp. 182-3.
[2] Law of 1692; Prov. Laws I. p. 63.
[3] This must not be interpreted as meaning that the towns no longer sought men
of proper religious qualification; but rather that there was no longer a narrow view of
what constituted the proper qualifications, and that the element of religion had lost its
dominance over other considerations.   The determination the religious qualifications
was not vested by this law in the ministry.   Yet, had it been, there would have been far
greater liberality than fifty years previous.   Law of 1701; Prov. Laws I. p. 470.
[4] Prov. Laws I. p. 681.
[5] Archer, in Standard Hist. of Essex Co., pp. 96-99.

and was part of the second parish of that town. Just how much
schooling its children had received in previous years cannot be
stated; most of it, however, had been furnished by private means.
Through agitation the town had given it a small amount of
the income from the school funds, which were unusually large,
in 1700, and possibly occasionally during the years thereafter.[1]
But there was no schoolhouse. The pastor, a Mr. Green, interested himself in the project of building one. The following
are extracts from his diary written on various days during March
1708: " 11th — I spoke to several about building a schoolhouse,
and determined to do it — 18. I wrote to ye neighbors about a
schoolhouse and found them willing to help — 22. Meeting of
the inhabitants. I spoke with several about building a schoolhouse. I went to ye town meeting and said to this effect, —
Neighbors, I am about building a schoolhouse for the good education of our children — and I speak of it here that so every one
that can have benefit, may have opportunity for so good a service. Some replied that it was a new thing to them and they
desired to know where it should stand and what the design for it
was. To them I answered that Deacon Ingersoll should give
land for it to stand on — and I designed to have a good schoolmaster to teach their children to read and write and cipher and
everything that is good. Many commended the design and none
opposed it." The pastor secured timber and built the schoolhouse hired the teacher and paid her himself for that year and
the next. It is probable that he received help from his neighbors,
but the work was to a large extent his alone. The general apathy
is apparent in non-opposition to the plan and in the failure to
help him in paying the school dame. His work bore fruit however. After this date town support seems to have been more
constant. In 1724 the school was held in four different places,
and in 1734 the whole amount spent upon schools in the town was
divided between the different parts of the town on the basis of
the Province tax.[2]

The second incident occurred in 1692 in Salisbury, which
town was probably not at that time compelled to support a grammar school. However that may be, the law was frequently if
not generally disregarded, and the character of the incident was
not affected thereby. The town in this year seems to have taken

(1) Felt, Salem I. p. 440.
(2) Ibid I. pp. 442-7.

an unusual action regarding schools. It is the motive of this action that interests us, for it indicates the new tendency of looking to the welfare of the individual as an individual and the consequent benefits to the community and the state thereby. The town voted to employ a teacher competent to teach Latin for the reason " that some young men wanted to be learned for a physician and a knowledge of Latin was necessary."[1] Whether the town was put to any additional expense in carrying out this act we do not know. But it does not matter, for it indicates the new point of view of the town looking primarily to the future of the individual and not to the perpetuation of the state.

Thus during the decades immediately preceding and following the year 1700 educational matters had reached a low level, but at the same time there was the beginning of a well-defined movement towards its upbuilding. This condition had been reached through several decades of growing indifference, and the improvement was destined to be even more slow. But the start was here made and at its inception was created the moving school.

[1] Currier, in Standard History of Essex Co., p. 405.

CHAPTER VIII

DECENTRALIZING TENDENCIES OF DEMOCRACY

The process by which the school broke away from the control of the church and became a civil institution has been traced in previous chapters. The changes in agencies of control from those created at the time of the establishment of the earliest schools to the close of the seventeenth century have also been set forth. The account was one of increasing democratization and secularization in the management of schools.[1] In this chapter it is desirable first to recapitulate in brief this entire development and to point out its bearing upon the creation of the moving school.

The transition of the school from an ecclesiastical to a civil institution took place during the first twenty-five years of the settlement. Before 1647 its establishment and maintenance were a blending of the old and the new forms of administration and support then used in schools and state. The practices of the church were most evident in the methods of supporting the master, while in the control of the school the civil agencies predominated. The powers of the civil agencies were, however, determined to some extent by the system of church administration. Their form as well as their powers, were very often influenced also by the method of administering chartered schools followed in England at that time. Both of these systems were aristocratic in tendency. As a result the selectmen or the board of feoffees probably exercised a larger amount of legislative control over the school than did the town meeting, and performed all of the executive functions as well.

In consequence of the passage of the law of 1647, the school came to be regarded wholly as an institution of the state and thus subject to civil methods of control and support. The voluntary contribution gave way to the civil tax; control by a permanent board of feoffees was largely abandoned, and the town meeting gradually assumed the legislative powers which legally belonged to it from the beginning.

---

(1) Chapters II and IV.

The latter half of the century stands out plainly as the era of the completely civil school. In form it was a school of a single teacher remaining in one place, usually in the village, which, however, was not always the geographical centre of the town. Those towns wherein democracy was strongest and those which were not fettered by any past practices soon developed the habit of performing all or most of the legislative functions necessary to the establishment and maintenance of the school in town meeting, and, thus, of delegating to the selectmen merely ministerial, or executive, powers. This system of school administration was universal at the close of the seventeenth century. There had appeared, however, at various times outcroppings of the still more democratic institution, the special temporary school committee, which was to have its period of rapid growth in the following century.

Thus, the development of school control during the entire seventeenth century may be characterized as an evolution of democratic and secular control out of the methods of control of church and chartered schools.

But the school constituted only one feature of the political administration of the town. While the experience in dealing with it doubtless had some effect upon increasing the power of democracy, yet the development of democracy in the control of other civil interests had a greater influence in the democratization and secularization of school control. The entire political movement was, moreover, a product of the changing social and economic life.[1] This background has been furnished in the preceding chapters. It remains here briefly to note the connection between the political and the social and economic life and to treat of these elements in the political life which made it possible for democracy to express itself in the making of new institutions. Then these institutions which had a direct effect upon the creation of the moving school must be described and their bearing set forth.

While on the one hand the loosening of the religious bond was causing the original society composed of its various ranks of ministry, gentry, and commonalty to fall apart, the difficult economic conditions with which they had to contend worked, especially in the rural towns, toward an equality—political and social,

[1] Chapters V and VI.

not absolute, but relative—among all men.[1]   This equality at the close of the century found its expression in a civil, not a church-state, and according to his abilities as a citizen in this civil state was each man regarded by his fellow man and given responsibilities in proportion thereto.

The performance of legislative functions upon the numerous and frequent questions which were brought before the town meeting in these communities, where seemingly almost everything that occurred in the public and private life of its inhabitants had to pass under the purview of the town meeting or its officials, gave all the inhabitants continuous exercise in the development of political sagacity.   The broad extent of New England functionalism developed this same quality in the administrative side of town government.[2]

Lengthening participation in the debates of town meetings and experience in office gave them also confidence in themselves — in the rightfulness of their opinions and in their ability to act upon their convictions.   The instinct of self-assertion in political affairs was approaching its maximum.   Each man wished to have the greatest amount of control through the realization of his ideas in legislation, and, if the duties of administration of that legislation were to his liking, in the actual executive control as well. His ideas of right were determined on the basis of selfish interest rather than upon the general welfare.   Each man desired to gain the maximum benefit of every civil enterprise.   And especially when his money went in the form of a town tax toward the support of any scheme or institution, he thought it right that he should get all the benefit from it that he could possibly secure.

What was true of the individual was likewise true of groups of individuals united by common selfish interests upon measures before the town meeting.   The sagacity and self-confidence of the individuals afforded a group sagacity and self-confidence which was more effectual in the gaining of their common ends.

In consequence, administration became decentralized.   Smaller geographical units were formed within the town.   The manner

---

[1] Weeden I. pp. 281-2. Just what was the effect upon the non-freeman in his participation in town affairs when colonial citizenship was bestowed upon him it is impossible to state. It seems, however, that it must have been in the direction of his greater self-assertion.

[2] Howard, pp. 96-99. Howard mentions some forty petty local offices which were established in different New England towns, many of which were held by several persons at the same time. In Manchester, in 1769, with 188 names on the tax list, 50 town offices were filled by the election of 36 men, 8 being elected to more than one office and three to four different positions. Manchester Records II. pp. 195-200.

and the extent to which democracy expressed itself in these subordinate organizations and their influence upon the moving of the town school now claim our attention.

Let us first take the parish, which was the earliest and the most prominent subdivision of the town throughout colonial history. As the population extended outward from the centre it became increasingly difficult to attend the services of the church located in the centre of the town. This was especially true in the case of a group of settlers on a fertile spot several miles removed from the central settlement or on the opposite side of a wide stream. Church attendance was most difficult in winter. Under such circumstances the need for a pastor among themselves was most apt to suggest itself and to meet with response from the town. Accordingly, even as early as 1650 some of these groups were permitted by the town to employ a minister for themselves either for part of or for the entire year, while they still remained members of the town church.[1] Some of these settlements became towns in a short time, others remained as parishes within the town; but in both cases these groups gained direct control of their church organization and also of the civil organization necessary to maintain the material interests of the church. By 1700 some twenty separate parishes had been constituted within the towns of which there were at that time eighty.[2] As many of these eighty towns were small, it follows that the parish was a well-recognized institution in the larger and more populous towns.

This indicates a strong tendency toward the division of local units to the smallest territory consistent with practicability. It was moreover deep-set in so far as churches were concerned. A reading of the town records at the time when a certain group of inhabitants wished to secure the consent of the town to the establishment of a new parish very often furnishes an account of a prolonged bitter quarrel, extending in some instances over many years and affecting the entire life of the town, public and private.[3]

The existence of the civil parish organization for the carrying on of the civil matters of the church with its full machinery [4] —

---

[1] Nason, Hist. of Beverly in Standard Hist. of Essex Co., pp. 68-71.
[2] Report of the Commissioner of Public Records 1885, pp. 10-148 passim.
[3] Currier's Newbury, pp. 347-8.
[4] Prov. Laws I. pp. 102, 506.

the parish meeting, clerk, constable, and assessors — presented constantly an administrative means for the accomplishment of this well-seated desire for divided control, and so emphasized the decentralizing tendency. The parish meeting became an organ for the discussion of the interests of the parish other than those connected with the church and for determining upon courses of action which should be taken to advance those interests.[1]

This extra-legal function of the parish demands our attention most particularly in connection with schools, in order that the effect of the manifestation of democracy through it upon the creation of the moving school may be judged. Springfield furnishes an interesting example.[2] In 1705 " the committee for the precinct on the west side of the great river in behalf of their said precinct did petition that the town would either erect and establish a school on their side......or else acquit them of paying any rate for the town school on the east side." In 1706 they again petitioned, at which time the privileges they desired from the town were obtained. Then the parish organization was used in the same way as the town government. It was agreed to and voted that " the said west side inhabitants have liberty to get a schoolmaster......and that the charge be carried on by the town in the same manner as the school affair is carried on on the east side of the great river according as the law directs."[3] By this, evidently, the parish, or precinct, was permitted to choose their own master; whether a committee of the precinct performed any part in the administration of the school in conjunction with the selectmen is uncertain. However this was the case in 1708, for it was voted that the " inhabitants of the said west side of the great river have liberty to add from among themselves some one man to join with the selectmen to carry on the affair."[4] Thus the parish became to some extent an agency in the administration of schools. As such, it was a subsidiary local unit for the execution of the state law, acting under the authority of the town in an extra-legal manner in the same way in which the school district later exercised these functions.

Similar conditions prevailed in what was known as Salem Village. In 1760 Salem granted fifteen pounds annually for

(1) Trumbull, Northampton II. pp. 194-8.
(2) Burt, Springfield II. p. 368.
(3) Ibid II. p. 372.
(4) Ibid II. p. 380.

three years to the inhabitants " without the bridge." One of the divisions of this territory was known as the " village " and later became Danvers. From that time on occasional grants were made. The administration of the school, which was part of the time entirely supported by the grant received from the town and part of the time by additional tuition, was carried on by the precinct organization. The first record tells of the choosing of three men as a school committee who were " empowered to agree with some suitable person to be a schoolmaster amongst us, in some convenient time, and make return to the people." The fact that the parish could not tax itself for additional funds to support its school was one of the principal reasons urged in the frequent petitions of the parish to be set off from Salem.[1]

The various precincts of Hadley exercised considerable power even from the beginning. In 1665 before the west side became a parish, it maintained its own highways and bridges. In later years the south precinct built its school house, and the east precinct administered the school funds given by the town and even taxed itself for support of schools.[2]

Muddy River, later Brookline, was in 1687 given independent powers of government in some respects and still held dependent to Boston in others. The " hamlet " was required to maintain its town highways and its own poor and to support a school. It held general meetings to carry on this administration and elected selectmen, surveyors, clerks, fence viewers, tithingmen, and a constable. It levied its own taxes for these purposes and enjoyed complete independence in control of its schools for some years.[3] While this was not a parish, yet to all practical intents and purposes, with the exception that it did not have a church, it may be regarded as of the same administrative rank. It shows the same general tendency of dividing and of including schools in the category of those concerns which the smaller and inferior unit should administer.[4]

Thus far our examples of the influence of democracy asserting itself through the parish toward the creation of the moving school have been confined to those cases wherein the

---

[1] Felt, Salem I. pp. 440-7. Archer, Hist. of Danvers in Standard Hist. of Essex Co., p. 99.
[2] Judd, Hadley, pp. 86, 403; Amherst Recs. p. 17.
[3] Brookline Recs. pp. 85-90.
[4] Worcester presents a similar case, the "North part" being set off in 1730 for seven years. Worcester Recs. II. p. 66.

precinct not only brought about the division of the school funds but also administered them to some degree, to a few corroborating instances of the extra-legal exercise of power, and to the independent power enjoyed by a local unit which was neither parish nor town. In each of these instances a divided and not a moving school resulted, meaning by this term a school taught by more than one teacher, each teacher teaching in only one place. In an ideal scheme of the evolution of the school district the divided school would be considered a later step than the moving school. Yet in some towns the moving school did not exist; in others it followed the divided school. The divided school must therefore be reckoned as one of the influences that worked towards the evolution of the moving school.

We shall now consider three instances in which the existence of the parish, or the agitation for its establishment, caused the erection of the moving school. In Newbury the first step for the erection of the second parish began in 1685. The contest waxed warm for years, the town refusing to consent until 1695 when the division was effected. In 1687 the first grant of money was made to each end of the town for a school. In 1691 was the first moving school. Then in 1693, when a compromise was effected by which the town supported a minister in the west end,[1] the aids given to education outside the centre ceased and was not resumed again until 1711, after which date it was continuous. Taking into account the feeling between the different sections of a town under stress of such a conflict between them, it is reasonable to conclude that the only way in which the vote for schools would be passed was through some such arrangement as this. Neither does it appear entirely a coincidence that the benefit extended to the outer parts of the town should be dropped when the parish was created. The inhabitants of the west end had gotten what they desired, they were not much interested in schools, the school was not entirely free from tuition except for the most elementary pupils, the tradition was in favor of the central school, and so they permitted the old order to be resumed.

In Watertown the decline in the intellectual spirit, combined with a slumbering dissatisfaction over the distance to the meeting

---

[1] Currier, Newbury, pp. 347-51.

9

house and school house, [1] accounts partially for the refusal of the town in 1690 to longer support a school by the town rate. Since the town would not vote sufficient funds for a school in the school house, the inhabitants were compelled to form a temporary association to complement the small amount granted by the town. But this arrangement soon failed. The school was not maintained according to law, and the town was presented to the court. When the law of 1701 increasing the penalty to twenty pounds was passed, the town was forced to support the school by a town rate and the only way in which this could be passed was to allow those in the west end of the town the school for one half the time. This arrangement was strictly maintained for years and the greatest care was exercised plainly that the interests of each side should be secured. Thus was created the moving school in response to the demands of the people who were petitioning that they should be made a precinct, and who had refused to longer vote sufficient money for a school in the village as had been done previously for over a score of years. The connection between the precinct and the moving school is obvious. [2]

In some, probably in most, towns the parish was created before the moving school. Thus the south precinct of Braintree was established in 1708, but it did not get any advantage from the town school until eight years later. Then it was given a reading and writing school at the expense of the town for one half year annually. This was in principle a moving school. For many years after the lines of division of the school were those of the parish. [3]

The Upper Society of Plymouth was formed in 1695 as the west precinct. In the following year was the first moving school in the town, being located in four places. While there is nothing beyond this single record to indicate connection between the two events yet it supports the evidence of the towns in which the relation is clear. [4] In Newbury it was customary to name in town meeting the various amounts that each parish should raise for the support of schools, and then the parishes appointed the

---

[1] These buildings were located in the easterly part of the town. The quarrel over the erection of another meeting house continued over thirty years.
[2] Drake, Hist. of Middlesex Co. II. pp. 407-8. Watertown Recs. II. pp. 26, 39, 42, 43, 62, 104, 108, 110, 126, 132, 139 et seq.
[3] Braintree Recs. pp. 70, 88 et seq.
[4] Plymouth Recs. II. p. 7, note; I. p. 245.

teacher and fixed the place or places where the school should be kept.[1]

Deerfield in 1740 and Sutton in 1745 present also instances of the parish being used as the territorial unit for the distribution of the moving school.[2]

The democratic impulse for maximum benefit and control took definite expression in strictly civil institutions as well. The most notable of these from the point of view of their influence upon the creation of the moving school and the later evolution of the school district was the division of the town into precincts for the repair of highways. The earliest records in many of the towns indicate a loose division of the town into parts and the election of one or more surveyors for each part. In Boston in 1636 two were chosen " for the highways towards Roxbury " and two " for the highways to the mill." In 1652 Rumny Marsh and Muddy River were each constituted a parish for a single surveyor.[3] Salem in 1644 elected two " surveyors of the highway towards the mill and the farms that ways " and two others for the highways " towards Wenham and that ways."[4] It seems likely that a similar method was followed in Dorchester also.[5] In Groton the " several squadrons " of the surveyors were definitely laid out by the selectmen within the first few years of the town's history.[6] In Watertown, however, the surveyors acted as a unit, while in Dedham both plans were used at various times.[7]

The evidence thus adduced seems to establish the conclusion that generally the different surveyors of highways directed their attention to different sections of the town. From what we know of the New England character it may be reasonably inferred that each surveyor had charge wholly or jointly of the section in which he lived. The town records from this earliest time do not furnish positive evidence of the continuation of this plan; their language is such as to make it possible that it did or did not exist. There are records, however, of action taken at the close of the century in the newly established Provincial Court

(1) Currier, Newbury, pp. 403-4.
(2) Sheldon, Deerfield I. p. 570. Benedict and Tracy, Sutton, p. 500.
(3) Boston Recs. II. p. 16; II. p. 108.
(4) Salem Recs. p. 130.
(5) Dorchester Recs. pp. 88, 98, 108.
(6) Groton Recs. p. 40.
(7) Watertown Recs. I. pp. 27, 125, 127. Dedham Recs. III. pp. 8, 97, 101, 105, 198.

and in the lately annexed town of Plymouth which go to show that it was perpetuated and that it was in general use at that time. The records of the town of Plymouth show from 1666 on that three or more surveyors were annually elected without anything being said as to assignment of definite territory. Then in 1700 after the surveyors were elected as usual it was voted that the town choose a committee " to settle how far each surveyor shall mend and survey," [1] as though no unusual action were being taken. It would seem upon the face of things that the town had become more fully settled so that the simple division of territory which had existed from the earliest days would no longer suffice, and that more definite and detailed bounds had become necessary.

The act of the General Court in 1693, [2] which was one of a series of acts that attempted to put into legal form the various previous enactments of the General Court and the local customs that had grown up under them, goes to show that the original practice still prevailed. It provided that two or more surveyors of highways should be chosen annually in each town, who were " to take care that all highways, causeys and bridges, lying within the precincts of such towns be kept in repair," etc. A later act passed in 1725 styled, " an act in explanation of, and in supplement to an act, entitled 'An Act for Highways, etc.'" gives us an insight into what was the condition of affairs at the time of its passage. After setting forth in the preamble a summary of the act it goes on to state in the same paragraph,— " but, forasmuch as there is no direction in the said act for stated limits to be observed by the surveyors in repairing and amending the said highways, and great inconvenience have happened or arisen in many towns;" it then enacts as a remedy for those conditions that the surveyors be assigned " their several divisions or districts for repairing or amending from time to time, all highways lying within the same."[3] These two acts taken together indicate in connection with the town records, that in 1693 it was the custom for the surveyors to have charge of certain roughly defined sections of territory, but that as yet in most towns either the road systems had not developed sufficiently to make a definite and extended distinction between

[1] Plymouth Recs. I. pp. 83-274 passim.
[2] Prov. Laws I. p. 136.
[3] Prov. Laws II. p. 338.

the sections necessary, or that the general laxity in the care of roads had not created the demand. It proves also that definite surveyor's districts existed generally after 1725.

The bearing of this upon the creation of the moving school lies in the fact that it predisposed people to division of the town schools. In fact in many respects the two subjects of highways and schools are alike in local administration. Today the school district and the road district constitute the two smallest divisions of local government. And here at the beginning we find them influencing the development of each other, as doubtless they have ever since. Their points of likeness to the farmer are that each takes his goods, either in time or money, and that neither will give him appreciable benefit in return unless the expenditure is made near to his door. Hence, the decentralizing tendency has ever been given a constant impetus in the administration of both institutions and the progress of one has naturally had the effect of increasing the momentum of the other.

Development of units within which all inhabitants contributed their common labor to the repair of all the highways within them began before the evolution of the school district. The inhabitants from the beginning worked only on roads near their homes; with the condition of the roads on the other side of the towns they were not concerned. With the dispersion of population and the increased age of the settlement, new roads were laid out and thus the burden of their care increased. It became necessary to make administration more certain and definite. The number of surveyors and so the number of districts were increased.[1] Units became smaller rather than larger, and as such they became well defined. To the extent that this division became conscious, to the same extent was strengthened the suggestion for the division of every benefit offered by the town's funds. And the school being peculiarly an institution from which they could not get full benefit unless it was brought close to them, the suggestion bore with particular emphasis upon it. Their political sagacity and strong self-confidence evolved when the time was ripe a plan wherein the previously undivided whole was broken up into parts and distributed among all the sections of the town, and with general satisfaction to all who were concerned.

---

[1] In Dorchester, in 1781, there were 2; in Braintree, in 1714, 4; in Boston, in 1690, 7; in Muddy River, in 1698, 3; in Groton, in 1671, 4; in Dedham, in 1705, 9; in Watertown, in 1694, 3; and in Plymouth, in 1700, 5.

It is impossible to state just how much weight the fact that the town was divided roughly into sections for care of roads, had upon the distribution of the school. We know that these divisions of the town existed in a rough manner and that the decentralizing tendency was generally manifest. On the other hand, there was little definiteness in the conditions, administration was loose, and little interest was taken in the care of roads. Yet there is no doubt that the system of road supervision precints did work toward the development of a group consciousness among smaller numbers and did therefore afford suggestions which lead to the creation of the moving school.

As compared with the parish, the highway surveyor's precinct had less influence in the rise of the moving school. The parish was a fully formed institution in constant activity. Moreover, it contained some of the most important features of the original town. Yet in the number of the places to which the moving school was sent neither the parish nor the surveyor's precincts seem to have been followed. Thus in Plymouth the school was held in four places and the number of surveyor's precincts was five, and the number of parishes two; in Watertown the numbers were two, three and two, and in Muddy River one, three and none, respectively. In Springfield the number of places was six, and the number of parishes three. In Manchester there was one parish, four surveyor's precincts and four dame schools. The records do not give satisfactory data, but on the whole it seems that the number of places in which the schools " went " lay between the number of parishes and the number of surveyor's precincts. On the whole, it seems probable that in the next century the number of schools approximated more nearly the number of surveyor's precincts.[1] The influence of both was toward division, but in the process of distributing the school, considerations which were peculiar to the school alone were given greatest weight.

Each of the great number of petty administrative civil offices created in consequence of the decentralizing tendencies was generally held by several individuals. In many cases it is clear that a division of territory more or less definite was made between

---

[1] The number of places in which school was kept in a town was probably, most frequently, four; the number of parishes was rarely over three and usually not over two.

them. With some offices this division tended to be definite and permanent; in others possibly there was no other division than that of relative convenience of residence to the work to be done among the different holders of the office. These all had a remote bearing upon the division of the school, their force being in proportion to the extent that each promoted group consciousness. They, therefore, deserve mention in this study.

The office in which division of the town's territory was most definite and in which case the bounds of the sections tended also to remain most permanent was that of the fence-viewer. His territory was more definitely marked off for him than was that of the surveyor of highways. It was thus from the beginning of the settlement to the close of the century.[1]

In consequence of the law of 1677, one tithingman was appointed to every ten families in the town. Division of territory [2] resulted. Hogreeves were likewise assigned to definite territory.[3] Some towns were divided geographically as a basis for determining membership in the companies of the militia. In Watertown there were three military precincts established in 1691, the bounds being approximately the same as those adopted later in the division of town into parishes and into sections in which the moving school was held.[4] In Plymouth the two companies were divided by a road running east and west and were known as the " Northerly " and " Southerly " companies.[5]

Division of families among the selectmen was suggested in the first law dealing with education in 1642. This often resulted in a division determined by the convenience of the selectmen, each taking families who resided near him.[6] This method of division is the only one set forth in the Connecticut laws of 1650 which is modelled after this law of 1642.[7] In Watertown in 1676, the selectmen went there " their several quarters to make trial " of children and servants.[8] In Cambridge, in 1671, the town was divided into eight distinctive precincts marked by definite bounds.[9]

(1) Dorchester Recs. pp. 99, 197, 276. Dedham Recs. III. p. 97; IV. p. 217. These references furnish typical cases.
(2) Mass. Col. Recs. V. p. 133; Boston Recs. VII. p. 138; Dorchester Recs. p. 223; Prov. Laws I. p. 680.
(3) Boston Recs. VII. p. 46; Plymouth Recs. II. p. 215.
(4) Drake, Hist. of Middlesex Co. II. p. 445.
(5) Plymouth Recs. I. p. 214.
(6) Mass. Col. Recs. II. p. 9; Hazen, Billerica, p. 252.
(7) Clews, Ed. Legislation and Administration of the Colonial Government, p. 74.
(8) Watertown Recs. I. p. 104.
(9) Cambridge Recs. p. 188.

Constables were also elected for definite divisions of the town. In Watertown in 1698 there were the first, second, and third constable, each for one of those divisions of the town which later became a parish.[1]   In Duxbury these divisions were called constablewicks.   The line dividing them was used in 1737 in the division of the town into sections for the apportionment of the moving school.[2]

Assessors were elected from different parts of the town also, as in Watertown in 1694, when there were " two of the East End, two of the township, and one of the Farms." [3]

An account of the development of the minor administrative districts in Boston reveals this tendency to subdivision very clearly.   In 1669 the town was divided into four districts for the purpose of securing better supervision of the swine.   Ten years later a town watch for fires was established.   Eight companies were created, one in each of the two " wards " in each of the four " quarters " of the town for this purpose.   This same territorial division was followed in the appointment of tithingmen one year later.   Eight constables were appointed the next year, whether one for each company is not clear.   The frequency of the election of four individuals or of a multiple of four after this date strongly suggests that these lines were followed more or less closely.   The term " ward " also began at this time to come into common use.   This also indicates definite division of the town.[4]   A similar tendency to elect officers from different fixed territorial sections of the town seems to appear also in Braintree after the division into parishes, in Watertown during the nineties, and in Billerica.[5]

At the close of the seventeenth century we find that the school was in control of a democracy which was with rare political sagacity and strong self-confidence demanding for the individual the maximum control of, and the minimum benefit from, all institutions to which the people contributed their support.   This political principle had led to the creation of additional parishes within the town, and to the division of the town into an increasing number of surveyor's districts.   Active participation in the

---

[1] Watertown Recs. II. p. 69.
[2] Duxbury Recs. p. 246.
[3] Watertown Recs. II p. 77.
[4] Boston Recs. VII. pp. 46, 131, 138, 143, 222.
[5] Braintree Recs., p. 81; Watertown Recs., pp. 69, 74; Hazen, Billerica, p. 190.

parish both in control and support of the church, and in the surveyor's precincts, emphasized the advantages of decentralization, and accelerated the movement. Furthermore, many of the town's administrative concerns were carried on by several officials in a single office with a division of territory amongst them. This policy had the effect of strengthening the suggestions afforded by the parish and the surveyor's precinct. It stood for a general habit of administration, that of establishing plurality where singularity might have sufficed, and of distributing the divided institutions over the various parts of the town. It was in response to this irresistible tendency toward maximum benefit and maximum control, as expressed in these various decentralized institutions, that, when the time came for increased attention to be directed to educational affiairs, the moving school was created.

CHAPTER IX

THE DAME SCHOOL

Alongside the system of public schools established in Massachusetts in 1647 there existed a series of private schools, not so well articulated nor so prominent, but yet occupying a large place in the life of the colony. They were, (1) the grammar school of a pastor of a church (2) the reading and writing school taught by a master, and (3) the dame school. The second and especially the third had an important bearing upon the transformation of the fixed or standing school into the moving school and must therefore receive our careful consideration. As there is more material at hand concerning the dame school, and as both influenced the creation of the moving school in much the same way, the process will be traced out in connection with the dame school. Then such facts as we have concerning the master's school which are of importance will be presented and their bearing shown in the light of the previous treatment of the dame school.

Family instruction was supposed in New England to furnish the fundamentals of education, and the parents were held responsible by the state for the training of their children, at least up to the point of the minimum standard laid down by law.[1] The civil school was established to promote education up to this point and to encourage the attainment of higher standards. But the establishment of the town school did not relieve the parents of the burden. If the parent did not send his child to the town school or if there was no town school to which to send him, he had to provide for the education of his child either in the family or in a private school.[2] From the standpoint of the state it made no difference which class of educational institutions was chosen, or whether the child went to school at all. Its only concern was the attainment of the minimum standard on the part of all, and the prevalence of a favorable disposition toward education among a sufficient number of the inhabitants to perpetuate the state upon its high intellectual, moral and, religious plane.

[1] Law of 1642; Mass. Col. Recs. II. p. 9.
[2] Dorchester Recs. p. 73; Judd, Hadley, p. 65; Watertown Recs. I. p. 105; Hazen, Billerica, p. 252.

The dame school, copied from England, owed its existence in Massachusetts primarily to the desire of parents to be relieved from part of the instruction of their children or else to place them in the hands of those whom they believed more competent to perform that service; and secondarily, to the failure of the civil school to furnish the grade of instruction carried out in it, and, in the case of girls, to admit them at all.

Similar reasons caused the existence of the private master's school for teaching reading, writing, and the elements of arithmetic. When there was no town school it furnished this higher grade of instruction, and when there was a town school it was held for the reason that it was more satisfactory to some parents, because of better instruction, greater convenience, or other reasons.

We turn now to the dame school. There is evidence of its existence from the beginning of the colony, though mention of it does not become frequent until toward the close of the century. From that time on through the whole of the eighteenth century it was common in the towns of Massachusetts except possibly in the smallest settlements.[1] Margery Hoar, the wife of the teacher and pastor of the church at Braintree is an example of a dame of the early time. She lived in this town from 1639 to 1687. She is described as being of an " amiable and good " English family, and as a " gentlewoman of piety, prudence, and peculiarly accomplished for instructing young gentlewomen, many being sent to her from other towns, especially from Boston."[2] This kind of dame school furnished an education for young ladies of a higher grade than that of the ordinary dame school. It is found existing in the same form throughout the eighteenth century but it had no appreciable effect upon the creation of the moving school.[3]

It is with the lower grade of dame schools, wherein the smaller children were taught their letters and to read and spell from their primers,[4] with which we are concerned in this study. Though they likewise probably existed from the beginning, we do not find mention of them until forty or fifty years after the first settlement. Possibly the deterioration of family instruction

[1] Corey, Malden, p. 631.
[2] Adams, Three Episodes in Mass. History,, p. 604.
[3] Trumbull, Northampton II. p.182; Boston Recs. XI. 172 et seq.; Hazen, Billerica, p. 257.
[4] Johnson, The Country School in New England, p. 25.

brought them into greater prominence, and possibly, also, the increasing distance from the town school and the corresponding decline in the amount of education received by the children elevated the importance of their instruction. Again, possibly, the difficulty of getting masters for schools caused more frequent use of the dame school,[1] and thus heightened its position in the communities so that the records of them are more frequent. In just what proportion these different factors entered in to emphasize the dame school, it matters little to our study. The facts are that at the close of the century the dame school seems to have existed generally. Of this we must now submit the proof in so far as this present study has brought instances of them to light.

The earliest mention of a dame school of this inferior class is found in Woburn in 1673. There were two schools during this year, one kept by " Allen Convar's wife " and the other by "Joseph Wright's wife."[2] There were one or more dame schools in this town from that date to 1680, and in 1686 also, and from this time on they were probably continuous. In Billerica in 1679 there were several school dames giving instruction, according to the report of the town to the General Court in 1679, which reads " As for schools we have no grammar scholars: ensign Thompson is appointed to teach those to write and read that will come to him: also several school dames."[3] In Concord in 1680 there were " in every quarter of our town men and women that teach to read and write English when parents can spare their children and others to go to them."[4] Cambridge in the same year had one school dame the record reading " For English, our school dame is goodwife Healy."[5] " Goodwife Merrick served in the same capacity in Springfield at about this time."[6] All of these references indicate that these schools had existed previous to this time but just how long cannot be said. In Andover during the latter part of the seventeenth and the early eighteenth century there were dame schools.[7] Samuel Sewall records in his diary under date of the twenty-seventh of April 1691 : " This afternoon had Joseph to school to Capt. Town-

---

[1] Bailey, Andover, p. 518.
[2] Sewall, Woburn, p. 52. The dames are usually referred to as the wife or daughter of some man.
[3] Hazen, Billerica, p. 193.
[4] Walcott, Concord, p. 129.
[5] Paige, Cambridge, p. 373.
[6] Green, Springfield, p. 183.
[7] Bailey, Andover, pp. 517, 518.

send's mother's his cousin Jane accompanying him; carried his horn book." [1] The "Diary and Letters of Thomas Hutchinson "[2] contain references to two dame schools kept in Boston in the second decade of the eighteenth century, one kept by a Mrs. Trivet, another by a Mrs. Wooddell, the age of the children going to them varying from three to seven years. The wife of Ebenezer Field, the smith of the town of Northfield, kept the first school known in that town in 1721. " She taught a class of young children at her own house, for twenty-two weeks of the warm season."[3] John Hartwell's wife was given leave " to keep a school to instruct children to read in Billerica in 1719."[4]

These references would seem of themselves sufficient to indicate the general existence of the dame school throughout the colony. In further support of this view we have, moreover, the statement of one who is known as having had an intimate and exact knowledge of local history of the towns of Massachusetts. Sylvester Judd, in his history of Hadley states, " There were many cheap private schools in Massachusetts and Connecticut in the seventeenth and eighteenth centuries kept by dames in their own rooms where girls were instructed to read and sew, and, in some, small boys were taught to read."[5]

Having established the general existence of the dame school, their location in the towns next claims our attention. It follows in the nature of things that the school must have been near to the homes of the children, for the children who attended these schools were young children of both sexes or older girls, and they could not go far. In those towns which by the close of the century had become scattered, some of the dames taught probably in the old centre and others in the outskirts of the town where the dwellings were somewhat closely situated. Upon this point explicit proof is meagre; such as it is will here be given. In Concord as we have seen, either a man or a woman was teaching " in every quarter of the town "[6] in 1680. In Woburn in 1673 there were two school dames paid by the town and so it may be inferred they were in different parts of the town.[7] Billerica in 1679 had " several dames and at the same time it had a writing

---

(1) Mass. Hist. Col., 5th series. V. p. 344.
(2) Pp. 40-46.
(3) Temple & Sheldon, Northfield, p. 163.
(4) Hazen, Billerica, p. 254.
(5) Judd, Hadley, p. 64.
(6) Wolcott, Concord, p. 129.
(7) Sewall, Woburn, p. 52.

and reading master which indicates their distribution over the town.[1] A like inference is to be drawn from the statement of the selectmen of Andover in 1713 " we do take the best care we can for to bring up our children to reading by school Dames."[2] In Northampton according to the statement of its historian there were in the early eighteenth century school dames in all sections of the town.[3] This evidence seems sufficient to prove the existence of dame schools in the outer sections of the town. As we go on to show the influence of these schools upon the creation of the moving school the point will be more strongly sustained.

At the beginning of the eighteenth century the educational process was carried on in those towns which maintained schools according to law by three different agencies — the family, the private school — chiefly represented by the dame school — and the town school. The town school, whether a grammar school purely, a combination of the grammar and reading and writing school, or a writing school simply, furnished instruction continuous to that offered in the dame school. In other words, the usual education furnished in the dame school was required for admission to the town school.[4] So when the parents wished to take advantage of the school for the education of their boys, they sent them first to the dame school in summer until they had learned to spell and to read their primers, and then to the town school.

These two facts stand out prominently in this scheme of education in a small town. First, as far as inferior education in the dame school was concerned all sections of the town were on an equality; second, that in the intermediate and higher education there was marked inequality in benefit. For this inequality, however, partial amends were made in the provisions for school support. This condition was tolerated because of the decline in educational interest and because of that combination of reverence for the wisdom of their forefathers and of the lack of initiative in all affairs, which caused them to hesitate to modify the established order. But when renewed activity sprang up in regard to

---

[1] Hazen, Billerica, p. 193.
[2] Bailey, Andover, p. 518.
[3] Trumbull, Northampton II. p. 182.
[4] Currier, Newbury, p. 396; Boston Records, XXXI p. 209; Worcester Records, Worcester Society of Antiquity Proceedings, 1879, p. 70.

education, and when they began to forge ahead on new paths, this contrast of equality and inequality in the two grades of schools was clear to those who were missing that benefit and they called loudly for its correction.

This sentiment naturally formed about the dame school as the institution for the inferior instruction. It served as a centre for the development of a group consciousness in regard to schools. The movement was accelerated by the other decentralizing tendencies in church and state. Its demand was, increased recognition from the towns for each particular group in educational administration. It took two forms — (1) for direct benefit from the town school by its being placed in each outlying section so that their children might have the same privilege of instruction in it as did the children of the centre of the town; (2) for town support of the dame school so that, by no longer having to support it for themselves, they might have some compensation for the disadvantageous conditions under which they found themselves. The second was seemingly a compromise; when granted it was but a question of time until the town school itself was placed in the group formerly ministered to by the dame school.

As the first was the cry usually of several groups, all of which were broadly on an equal footing, and as the centre constituted under normal conditions far the largest group, it became necessary for the outlying sections to unite upon a platform upon which they could all stand in opposition to the strong centre. This was, naturally, equal benefit from the school for all the sections and this meant dividing the term into as many parts as there were groups of people and moving it around from section to section until the entire circle was complete.[1]

Having described the process, it remains to show how it worked out in concrete instances. We shall first give examples of the first mentioned form which the demand took — namely the direct creation of the moving school; and then of the second — the support of the dame school by the town, followed later by the moving school. Owing to the incompleteness of our knowledge

---

[1] The fact that the division would give them the benefit of the school for but a short time was not an objection to those living in the outer sections. Their Dame School was kept during the summer only, and their reading and writing school, if they had one, for not more than three months; and if there was no private master's school in their midst, the time the moving school would be in their section would probably be as long as the time most of the children attended it in the town at far greater inconvenience. The outer sections were the gainers in all cases.

of the details of the early history of these towns, each of the two classes of examples has a general defect. In the former we are unable to state positively except in one instance that there were private dame schools in the outer sections of the town, corresponding somewhat in number and location to the places to which the moving school was sent, although we know there were several dame schools situated at some points in the towns. In the latter class of towns, we know that the number and location of the public dame schools correspond very closely to the number and location of the moving school as it was sent on its rounds, but we do not know positively of the existence of the private dame school at any place in the town previous to the time that they received town support. There seems to be no reason, however, why we cannot permit the deficiency in the one case to supply that in the other. For the private dame school was universal — as the school that gave the inferior instruction necessary to admission to the town school. It must have existed prior to the time it was incorporated in the town school, and it must have existed in almost the same way in which it was incorporated — that is in groups of families forming more or less defined sections.

Beginning with the first class of towns, those which show the direct establishment of the moving school without the intervening step of the incorporation of the dame school into the town system, Woburn furnishes a typical instance.

Woburn we know had town dame schools from 1673 to 1694, and its histories say there must have been private " women's schools " or dame schools during the early part of the eighteenth century. The town school was kept intermittently from 1686 to 1701 and after that date regularly. In 1706 it became a moving school. In this case we lack positive evidence of dame schools in the outskirts of the town but it may be fairly assumed that there were such as the order making the grammar school a moving school gives us the following reason for the action : — " Forasmuch as our town of Woburn is situated very scattering and remote, so that the whole town cannot be benefitted alike ; " some of the dames must have lived in these scattered parts.[1]

Billerica in 1679 stated in its report to the General Court that it had " also several school dames." In 1717 or thereafter the

---

[1] Sewall, Woburn, pp. 52, 210, 211-13; 229, et seq.

school was moved into the " several quarters " of the town, " to accommodate outskirts of the town."[1] There is every reason to believe that the conditions were no different here than in Woburn.

Andover from 1700 on generally had a grammar school. School dames also kept school we know by the fact that the town reported to the Court in 1713 when they were unable to secure a master that " we do take the best care we can for to bring up our children to reading by school dames." In 1719 the school was made a moving school, being held at first in each of the two precincts, and later in 1729 going into three different places but moving six times in the year.[2] But here again there is lack of absolute proof that there were dames in the outer sections.

In Brookline this difficulty does not appear. Since 1686 there had been from time to time standing schools for teaching reading and writing, and most probably school dames as well. In 1710 the town passed the following order : — " That there be liberty granted to erect two school houses at their own charge that improve them. Also that they maintain a good school dame half of the year at each house. That the town allow the charge for a master one quarter at one school house and the other quarter at the other. To teach, to write and cipher."[3] Here there is no question that the private dame schools were maintained in parts of the town, and that their number and location corresponded to the place in which the moving school was held. That the dame school was a factor in bringing about the moving school — that it was a centre for group feeling and action respecting schools — there can be no doubt.

We turn now to the class of towns in which the answer to the demand for greater equality in the enjoyment of the privileges of the town school first took the form of town support for the dame school in the outer sections, the moving school following a few years later. Manchester furnishes an instance of slow evolution. The year 1696 gives us the first record of a town school. It was of the prevalent kind — the standing school. The next record is of the year 1718, when both a master and a dame were ordered hired by the town — possibly the first for winter, the second for summer ; but it was still the standing school. From this time on to 1735 it is quite difficult to tell whether this arrangement was continued. Part of the time, as in 1727, refer-

---

(1) Hazen, Billerica, pp. 252-5.
(2) Bailey, Andover, pp. 517-20.
(3) Brookline Recs. pp. 77, 96.

ence to a master only is made, in 1728 to a " master or masters ; " and in 1732 and 1733 the tax is levied for the support of a " free school or schools." Thus there may have been a moving school previous to 1635. In that year it was voted to maintain a standing master's school in the school house during the fall and winter and four dame schools, " one in that part of our town called Newport, one in that part lying near the meeting-house and one in that part called the plain, and one in that part of our town called Cettel Cove." This arrangement prevailed up to 1738. In that year it was voted that the master's school " be removed to the four quarters of the town, they in each part to provide a suitable house — and the time and place at the discretion of the selectmen." While these records do not give proof of several private dame schools yet the fact that a dame was employed part of the time in the standing town school indicates their existence. The influence of the existence of the dame school upon the creation of the moving school is clear.[1]

Worcester from the time of the first record concerning a school in 1726 maintained a standing school taught wholly by a master until 1731. In April of that year it was ordered that " whenever many small children cannot attend ye school in ye centre of ye town by reason of ye remoteness of their dwellings and to intent that all children may have ye benefit of education, etc.

" Voted that a suitable number of school dames not exceeding five be provided by ye selectmen at ye charge of ye town for ye teaching of small children to read, and to be placed in ye several parts of ye town as ye selectmen may think most convenient." The reading and writing school was ordered continued as formerly in the centre of the town until the next September. Then at the town meeting in that month it was voted that this school " be a moving school into the several quarters of the town."[2] Here the steps were taken in quick succession. This fact served to make the influence of the private dame schools in the various sections of the town immediate and direct ; though probably the experience of the people with the public dame schools during the intervening summer played some part in strengthening the tendency toward equalization of school benefits.

[1] Manchester Recs. I. pp. 70, 143, 144, 150, 170, 175, 180 187, 191, 198; II. pp. 22, 23, 26.

[2] Worcester Recs. 1879, pp. 39, 48, 49, 59, 62, 66, 70, 73.

Besides these two classes of towns there is another which is characterized by a combined influence of the dame school and the parish in causing the creation of the moving school. The inhabitants in the western part of Newbury began in 1685 to petition the town to employ a pastor for them. In 1687 the town voted five pounds " to each end of ye town " for a master's school. In 1691 the town school was moved into three places. That there were private dame schools in the town, is shown by the fact that three years later a company of six men were granted land upon which to build for themselves a school house " for the accommodation of a good and sufficient school dame." Undoubtedly there were other dames teaching children of other groups, but for whom there did not appear the necessity of asking a grant of land for the building of a house or any other favor from the town.[1]

Deerfield established a standing master's school in 1698, and maintained it thus to 1728. In that year permission was granted to all farmers to procure school dames, which we know to have been keeping school as early as 1694, to teach their children until October 15th, and a grammar school was ordered from that date until the first of the next April. This scheme seems to have been followed in all parts of the town, except that which later became Greenfield, until the time of the division of the town into districts in 1787. In 1732, however, specific provision is begun for a school dame at Green River. This continued until 1740 when the master's school was moved to Green River for " their proportionable part of the year." Here, evidently, were private dame schools which were the centres of group consciousness regarding schools, creating a sentiment for division of school privileges and operating with the parish sentiment in securing the moving of the town school for part of the year.[2]

This is also an example of the influence of the dame school upon the establishment of the "divided" school. It is noteworthy also for the fact that here all the steps of the evolution are complete,—private dame school—public dame school, divided school, and in a partial manner, the moving school.

Of the private reading and writing schools less is known. Histories of the towns of less than fifty householders at this

(1) Currier, Newbury, pp. 399-401.
(2) Sheldon, Deerfield I. pp. 272-4, 570; II. pp. 839-40, 842.

time assert the existence of schools previous to a record of their maintenance by the town, basing their assertions presumably upon the known interest of the people in education and the fact that they were supported without the town rate.[1]   Thus Newhall in his history of Lynn concludes there must have been a school in Lynn about 1642 and during the intervening period to 1691, when there is a record of the town choosing a master. Lewis in his annals of the same town states " Mr. Shepherd kept the school several months this winter.— A month or two in the winter, under the care of the minister, was the principal opportunity that they had to obtain the little learning requisite for their future life." [2]   Likewise Bailey's Andover asserts that the ministers kept the first schools and down to 1700.[3] An account of the school in Concord previously quoted states: " as for schools we have in every quarter of our town men and women that teach to read and write English when parents can spare their children and others to go to them." [4]

That " there were usually some men and some women with sufficient education to teach the rudiments — who could receive scholars at their homes and charge two pence to six pence for instruction " at the time of the first settlement of the town is the statement made by a writer of several town histories.[5]   These schools referred to above were probably all reading and writing schools (except the dame school in the last reference).   It is to be noted that these were held in the winter time and likely most often in the large well-warmed kitchen of a private house.[6] When the town had grown sufficiently to come under the operation of the law, we then find sometimes, as in Billerica, that they made a private master, the town's schoolmaster, though he drew no pay from the town.[7]

Record of the existence of private reading and writing schools are found in the larger towns contemporaneously with town schools. In Boston in 1667 " Mr. Will Howard was granted liberty " to keep a writing school to teach children to write and keep accounts," and in the following year Mr. Robert Canon

[1] Sewall, Woburn, p. 51.
[2] Newhall, Lynn, pp. 203, 292; Lewis, Lynn, p. 170.
[3] Bailey, Andover, p. 517.
[4] Wolcott, Concord, p. 129.
[5] Temple, North Brookfield, p. 199.
[6] Ibid, p. 199.
[7] Hazen, Billerica, pp. 193, 253.

was "licensed to keep school." In 1712, the year a law was passed by the General Court requiring that the teacher of private schools receive the approval of the selectmen,[1] three masters and one mistress were permitted to continue, stating in two of the cases, " as they have heretofore done." Mention is made of them in Salem and Boston frequently after this time.[2] The fact that there were private schools in Boston, and possibly in Salem, during this time gives confirmatory evidence of their existence in other towns as well.

The influence of these reading and writing schools upon the creation of the moving school was the same in kind as those of the dame school. It may have been greater in degree for the reason that it was the same grade of school as that maintained by the town, and the custom of keeping such a school in the outer sections of a town would produce a stronger feeling and a more persistent action in securing equality of benefit from the town school. But on this point we do not have sufficient material to form a judgment.

The cases wherein this effect is shown are not complete in a single instance. All of them are like the second class of cases presented under the dame school, and do not show the existence of the private schools before their incorporation into the town school. It cannot well be doubted in the light of what has already been said in this chapter, however, that they existed. The cases are also few in number. This is as would be expected. When the town school of the same grade was established, the natural tendency would be for the children to go to them, and for the private reading and writing school to cease, except in those towns where there were exceptional conditions.

Newbury from 1652 to 1687 maintained only a standing master's school. In that year as has just been noted in the discussion of the dame school the inhabitants provided for schools at " the ends." The fact was not emphasized there, however, that these schools were to be taught by masters " for ye teaching of children to read, write and cipher." Four years later the school was made a moving school.[3]

---

(1) Prov. Laws I. p. 681.
(2) Boston Recs. VII. pp. 36, 43; Boston Rec. XI. pp. 165, 172, et seq.; Felt, Salem I. p. 442, et seq.
(3) Currier, Newbury, p. 400.

Lunenberg had its first town meeting in 1728, but no action was taken concerning schools until 1732. Then it was voted to have a school kept by a master to teach reading and writing, or a grammar school master in case the additional charge was met in some other way. But instead of this school there seems to have been four schools kept by masters, for at the next March meeting four men were ordered paid for keeping school in the town small amounts varying from thirteen shillings to three pounds. The next winter there was a town reading and writing school for three months. In the following year a moving school was ordered to be kept in three places " by some suitable person at such price as ye said committee shall agree for." In 1736 dame schools were ordered " as they [the selectmen] shall see meet." [1]

In Sutton the schools kept by the masters do not appear until after the standing school, but no doubt they were a survival of the earlier time. The first school in 1730 was a moving school, held in four places, one month in each. In 1731 school dames were supported by the town. In 1733 there was a standing town school; in the following year, three men were paid for teaching one month each, and the master for the previous year was paid for a time not specified. Probably he taught for a longer period. By the next year he had risen to the dignity of " ye town's schoolmaster." In 1737, if not before, the school became a moving school again. [2] The influence of the private masters school upon the founding of the moving school is here very plain.

In conclusion, it is to be noted that in those towns where the reading and writing masters were found, that there were also school dames. This indicates the relationship of the two institutions to each other and their common relationship to the town school when they were located in the outer sections of the town. The dame school was the summer school; the master's school, the winter school, of these people. They gave birth to the same thoughts, feelings, and actions in regard to sharing in the town school, to the support of which the people contributed, and in determining the place where the moving school should be held. Of all the decentralizing tendencies then working in Massachu-

---

(1) Lunenberg Recs. pp. 77, 79, 83, 85, 94. The use of the word "person" permitted the employing of either a master or a dame. Its use is significant for this reason whenever met with in the records.

(2) Benedict & Tracy, Sutton. pp. 499-500.

setts society this was probably the most powerful though not the most immediate in producing the moving school.[1]

[1]Of all the towns referred to in the previous chapters, and not in this, some never had a moving school, but established the divided school at the beginning of their modification of the central standing school. This was true in Springfield, Salem, Northampton (the school in the South parish was moved), and Boston. In Braintree and Plymouth the situation is involved, but the influence is clear. In Dedham and Watertown no evidence of the influence of the private schools has been found. The records of some other towns cease before the erection of the moving school, and of others the town histories which have been used on other questions cannot be depended upon here. To this class belong Dorchester, Ipswich, Charleston, and Cambridge.

CHAPTER X

THE ABOLITION OF THE TUITION-TAX

The last years of the seventeenth century and the first of the eighteenth were the " dark days " of New England. It was the time when the intellectual and educational life reached its lowest ebb. The principles and the spirit of the earliest settlers had gradually lost their hold upon society during the preceding fifty years and as yet no new influence had come in to guide and animate its life. It was also a time of war; the resources of the colony were sapped almost to exhaustion; the lives of many of the men were sacrificed in battle; and commerce and industry were sadly interrupted. In the midst of this low and discouraging condition of affairs, a change in the form of political government was made. This was not, however, to them a wholly unmitigated evil. For by it permanency and security in the relation to the mother country was gained; and the liberty of self-government was not interfered with to any great extent.

There were, however, in the midst of this low condition of affairs, signs of the upward movement. In the realm of education, it first appeared in a few hours and gradually widened until it had gained sufficient strength to secure the passage of laws by the provincial legislature. With these laws as a coercive force it was not long until all but the smallest of the towns felt its influence. There was then produced an educational revival, not in the extension or the enrichment of the curriculum but in the spreading of benefits of the existing curriculum to all the children. Not this alone, however, for in this same revival the privileges of an education in a state elementary school free of tuition charge was secured to every child. These two results were in many towns a joint product of the same movement. Low social and economic conditions compelled the abandonment of the tax on scholars and entire support by the town rate; this in turn brought about the creation of the moving school. To understand this step, we must know the process from its beginnings. This chapter is an attempt to present this educational revival in so far as the elements of school support and its effect upon the exterior form of the school are concerned.

The educational revival began to appear locally in a few towns as early as 1680. Boston in 1683 established in addition to its town grammar school two town reading and writing schools in different parts of the town. These were free to all the children of the town, although it was urged that " such persons as send their children to school (as are able) should pay something to ye master for his better encouragement."[1] Two years previous Salem received the first of her large gifts from several members of the Brown family, part of which, if not all, were intended to lessen the cost of the charges made upon the pupils for attendance. By 1712 a number of other gifts and bequests had been made in the support of a writing school which was established in that year. Dedham in 1680 was presented with sixty pounds to be used as an endowment in the support of its Latin School.[2]

It was not until 1701 that the movement had gathered sufficient strength to secure legislation of a really mandatory character through which means every town large enough to have a school could be reached. A penalty of a fine was provided for in the very first legislation upon schools in 1647.[3] In 1671 [4] the fine of five pounds for neglect in cases of both grammar and reading and writing schools was increased to ten pounds in the case of the former. The reenactment of the original laws in 1692 [5] fixed again the penalty for both kinds of schools at the same amount, and in doing so reduced the amount of the penalty imposed upon towns of two hundred householders.[6] The law of 1701 [7] doubled the penalty for both schools. Twenty pounds was almost sufficient to pay the wages of a reading and writing master for an entire year; and it was a considerable share of the annual wage necessary to secure a grammar master. The law was, in effect, mandatory. Furthermore the vigilance of the courts of quarter sessions seems likewise to have been increased at the same time. The result was a more effective administration of the central government. Seventeen years later it became necessary, however, to still further increase the penalty on towns having 150 householders and over, the amount increasing with

[1] Boston Recs. VII. p. 161.
[2] Felt, Salem I. pp. 435, 436, 439, 440-2, 443, 445, 446-7; Dedham Rec. V. p. 98.
[3] Mass. Col. Recs. II. p. 203.
[4] Ibid IV. Pt. I. p. 486.
[5] Prov. Laws I. pp. 62-3.
[6] Law of 1683, Mass. Col. Recs. V. p. 414.
[7] Prov. Laws I. p. 470.

the population, at the rate of ten pounds for every fifty house-holders.[1]

This legislation caused in many towns a change in the manner of raising the master's wages. The intellectual decline and the distance the children on the outskirts had to travel, the presence of the dame schools, which furnished the rudiments of an educa-tion, and of the private master's schools in the outer sections, the dissensions and quarrels among the people, and the strong self-assertion of the individual in the democratic town meeting had all developed an indifference to the town school. It became more difficult to get the town rate voted; on the other hand, there was opposition to the payment of tuition upon the part of those who had to come far and a total lack of attendance on the part of some from all over the town because of the expense involved, so that it became increasingly difficult to get a sufficient amount of money from all sources to employ a master. This was all the more difficult by reason of the fact that at this time masters properly qualified and satisfactory to the court were scarce and in conse-quence were able to hold out for high wages. This inability to get funds wherewith to pay the master by the use of the old method of a combined town rate and a tax on the scholars who attended, forced its abolition, and the substitution of the town rate alone. But the price of this was the establishment of the moving school. The opposition to the town rate, not taking into account the opposition which always comes from the selfish property holder who has no children or from those who are opposed to schools, came from those who lived in the outer sections. The reason was that they did not get proportionate benefit in return. The partial payment of the master by tuition was in its effect a concession to this inequality. But it was not sufficient. To get the vote of the outer sections for a long time for the school rate, it was necessary that a scheme be devised whereby they could participate more directly in its benefits. On the other hand, the strong sense of justice which was developed by the constant assertion of the selfish interest caused those liv-ing in the centre to appreciate when the town rate alone was adopted, as they had not before, the right of the outer sections to easier access to the privileges of the town school. Hence the practical sagacity of the democratic assemblies formed the new

[1] Prov. Laws II. p. 100.

institution — the moving town school, going into all the parts of the town in such manner as would give greatest benefit to the greatest number.

This process as it evolved in the various towns must now be traced. Boston is to be excluded from its operation at once, for the reason that its interests as a commercial and industrial town unified its political and social life, and its concentrated population did not make a demand for the moving school. Its more lively interest in educational matters likewise prevented the keeping of schools for a short term. The same is to be said of Salem. In Boston, moreover, the main support of the school had been mainly by rate for many years. However, both towns recognized the justice of the demand of those who inhabited the agricultural regions of their towns for separate schools about the year 1700: Boston, for Muddy River, or Brookline, Rumney Marsh, and the North End; Salem, for the Village, Ryall Side, and the Middle Precincts.[1] In these actions the workings of the same principles as those which caused the moving schools in the rural towns is observed, though here the major force was the element of justice in the people of the centre rather than that of the selfish demand of the other sections.

There are two towns which present the working of the process in the clearest manner; one, a town which paid little or no attention to schools in an early day; the other, a town which maintained its school regularly for years, but later allowed it to lapse into decline. As the former is probably more typical of the majority of the towns, its development will be given first.

The first record of a town school in Malden [2] is found in the court records of Middlesex County. In 1671 the town was presented for not maintaining a school according to law. However, its committee satisfied the Court and the complaint was dismissed. The first mention of the school in the town records is under the date of 1691, where it reads, " Ezekiel Jenkins continuing to be the town's schoolmaster." In 1697 " John Moulton chosen schoolmaster " is the record, while that of two years later reads, " John Sprague chosen schoolmaster for this present year; for one year. It is left to ye selectmen to agree with him what

(1) Boston Recs. VII. p. 240; Felt's Salem I. p. 440.
(2) Corey, Malden, pp. 601-24.

he should have for his encouragement to keep school for one year." The absence of any mention of money to be paid him by the town except in the last case shows clearly that this was an instance where a private schoolmaster who got his pay from the scholars direct by way of tuition was by the town's act from time to time made the town's schoolmaster, thus enabling the town to comply with the law and without changing the character of the support.[1] The " encouragement " indicates the failure of tuition to give the master sufficient return to secure his services. It was not looked upon so much as a salary as a gift. Its purpose was to make him more inclined to keep school for an income which his calculations led him to believe would come in from tuition. The town extended it to him for the reason that it had to satisfy the law. Support by tuition alone failed.

Apparently John Sprague continued the school for two years. Then the town permitted the school to cease for some time, for, in December, 1701, the town was again presented " for ye want of a schoolmaster."

The school was not discontinued because the master was unsatisfactory, but because of the difficulty of coming to an agreement on salary. Either the master's previous income from the combined " encouragement " and the tuition of scholars was insufficient and he demanded an income which the town was unwilling to pay, or the town refused to give him longer the same amount and he refused to teach for less. Which of these was true will appear in the reading of the next act of the town.

But the town escaped the payment of the fine by employing Mr. Sprague before the case was called. Evidently the town was compelled to accede to his terms for the record of the court states that the selectmen " informed the Court that they have agreed with John Sprague till next March. The Court accepts him and dismissed paying fees." This agreement has not been preserved, but the act passed by the town the following March reveals its nature as well as the agreement for the year ensuing. It tells us, also, why Malden had been without a master for a time. " John Sprague is chosen schoolmaster for ye year ensuing to teach children to read and write and to refmetick accord-

---

(1) This arrangement would not be possible where there were poor children unless the master was charitably inclined, which is not at all improbable in many instances, or unless it was the custom of the town to let the well-to-do parents pay for the education of the children of the poor, not specifically, but by paying the higher tuition demanded of them by the master on account of his teaching the poor.

ing to his best skill. And he is to have ten pounds paid him by ye town for his pains. The school is to be free for all ye inhabitants of this town......" This leaves no doubt that the previous method of support of combined town tax and tuition had not provided sufficient funds and that the master was demanding more from the town, which increase the town refused to give.

The combined town tax and tuition had failed to afford a legal school. It was succeeded by the town rate alone, the legal character of which could not admit of failure.

But not all the record of the town's act in this annual meeting in March 1702 was quoted. The part which follows sets forth the change that it was necessary to make in the exterior form of the school in order to pass the school rate in the town meeting. The record continues from the point where it was interrupted in the preceding paragraph (repeating the last clause) " The school is to be free for all ye inhabitants of this town: and to be kept at four several places one quarter of a year in a place: In such places where these five men shall appoint, namely — [the five men are here named]......: who are chose by ye town for that purpose." It is evident that the town saw that it had to have a school in order to escape paying the twenty pound penalty, that in order to have a legal school it had to pay the master's wages by a town rate, and in order to carry the town rate it was necessary to grant to the inhabitants living in the outer sections of the town direct and easy benefit from the school for their children. The outer sections had undoubtedly said " If we pay as great a proportion of the support as the centre, we are entitled to a proportionate return from the school. We shall not vote the tax unless it is agreed to locate the school so each section may for part of the year enjoy as easy access to the school as any other section." And the inhabitants of the centre were forced to yield. Thus the abandonment of the partial support of the master by tuition produced the moving school.

The way in which the town administered its school after this date still further confirms this conclusion. In the following year the inhabitants succeeded in finding a man who would teach on the old plan of support. This method enabled the town to escape the payment of the fine at a less cost to itself, so the combined forces of those that were opposed to public expenditure for the support of schools, and of those in the centre who wished the best educational advantages for their children (it is difficult to state which motive was the stronger) won the day and, as the record reads, " Ezekiel Jenkins is chosen schoolmaster for the present year: and the school to be kept at his own house; he to have three pounds for ye year; and ye benefit of ye scholars." The week previous it had been voted " that ye school shall be kept in ye watch-house for this year." It may be assumed, therefore, that his residence was near the centre of the town. The following year his pay from the town was reduced to thirty shillings. He remained as master until his death in 1705, when Nathaniel Waite was chosen on the same terms. He continued to serve for small payments from the town and the " benefit of the scholars " to 1709, although at one time there was apparently a refusal to teach on his part which caused the town to be presented again. Then another offer was made to get John Sprague to teach, but he refused unless paid by town rate. In 1709 another master was chosen, to receive only two shillings from the town; and in the following year a man was found who agreed to teach for the tuition alone and he was accordingly elected. Evidently he was just the kind of a man for whom they had been long seeking. All of these masters taught in the centre of the town, and the amount of the town rate was small. Under such conditions the outer sections could not demand the school for a part of the time.

But the town was in 1710 compelled to return to the plan of 1701. Moses Hill who had agreed to keep the school for the benefit of the scholars alone found it not a paying venture. The town was presented to the Court of Quarter Sessions and ordered to get a master before the next meeting of the Court. Within ten days after the order of the court the town met and elected Nathaniel Waite master and " voted that the school shall be removed into three parts of the town, the first half in ye centre, and one quarter in ye southwardly end and one quarter in ye northwardly end of ye town." But the town would not agree to Waite's proposition. Another meeting under the pressure of apprehension of the fine was held two days later. The master elected refused to accept. They failed also in their third attempt. Finally a master was secured at a salary of sixteen pounds and ten shillings for six months, the school to be held in two places. A few days later the selectmen again appeared before the court, " exhibiting a note under ye hand of Mr. Samuel Wigglesworth " [the master] and, their report being accepted, they were dismissed. The town had learned a lesson from the Court and thereafter a stated provision by town rate was made for the school and nothing more is heard of the " benefit of scholars." The moving school was likewise thereafter a permanent feature of their school administration. There is no doubt that the same principle worked in this action as in that of 1701 — the demand for the return from the money voted for schools by those in the outer sections of the town.

In 1667 [1] the school of Watertown was made free to all the inhabitants of the town. Mr. Richard Norcross, who had been the master since 1651, was in that year paid thirty pounds a year out of the town rate. He continued teaching at the same salary until 1675, when his long service suffered its first interruption. In that year Mr. Goddard kept the school at the same wage.[2] Not all the elements in the controversy, which now occurred, can be ascertained. However, the question of the kind of school, the amount of salary, and the personality of different teachers seem to be some of the elements involved. The first two are of interest to us in this study for there was seemingly an effort to do away with instruction in Latin, a thing they could not do without violating the law. There was also an effort to get a master for lower terms and also to change the character of support. All of these tendencies are easily understood and are to be accounted for by the decline in the interest in education and the stringent economic conditions of the times. People were beginning to venerate less the old curriculum; they had of necessity become very frugal. They were coming to the conclusion that those who pursued Latin should pay for it themselves and that the town should no longer bear that charge. This growing sentiment probably accounts for the failure to hire Mr. Norcross any longer and for the irregular actions of the town for the succeeding five years. These years now require more definite notice.

After Mr. Goddard had served his year ending about May first 1676 at thirty pounds, no action was taken regarding schools until the next November, when it was " left with the selectmen to agree with a schoolmaster as cheap as they can."[3] There is no record of a master being hired, however. The discussion regarding the

---

[1] Watertown Recs. I. p. 91.
[2] Ibid I. p. 123.
[3] Ibid I. p. 127.

method of paying the master's salary was evidently rife during the winter for the question was voted on in the succeeding March when "the town declared by a vote that they would have the school kept a free school as formerly."[1]   The school was an English school and the salary of Lieut. Sherman, the master, was twenty pounds.[2]   Nevertheless Mr. Goddard seems to have continued as the grammar master with a small stipend from the town. We cannot solve the intricacies of the record further. In 1680 the warrant for the town meeting read — "to call ye town together so ye town may come to some loving agreement and conclusion about a schoolmaster."[3]   During that year Lieut. Sherman's school, presumably an English school merely, was the only one held.   In the following year it was ordered by the town that the committee chosen by the town secure a schoolmaster outside the town "that may answer ye law" and the trouble seems to have come to an end.[4]

The result of this period of turmoil was a decline in the amount, and a slight change in the method, of support. The school was still maintained as a grammar school so as to comply with the colonial law.   Incidentally, it is to be noted that Mr. Norcross again took up his old duties, though we can judge with little or no kindly feeling, for he must have felt keenly the change that was coming over the people since the early days and their apparent ingratitude to him for his long labors.   Furthermore, it was a changed regime in which he was now entering, and he must have foreseen it and dreaded the consequences it might bring forth.   The committee not being able to find any master out of town, the town-meeting of next August (1681) elected Mr. Norcross, agreeing to give him twenty-five pounds out of the town rate instead of thirty as formerly, but in addition "he was to have benefit of ye Latin scholars over and above said twenty-five pounds, and that to be as ye parents or governors of said Latin scholars and Mr. Norcross can agree — and said Mr. Norcross do engage to save ye town harmless from fine — [until time for his year proper to begin] — by teaching such Latin scholars as shall be sent to his house."[5]   That is, the town refused longer to support the grammar school proper, although

(1) Watertown Recs. I. p. 128.
(2) Ibid I. p. 129.
(3) Ibid I. p. 144.
(4) Ibid II. p. 8.
(5) Ibid II. p. 9.

the instruction in the elementary subjects was paid wholly by town rate as before. It is also evident that the town provided a man who could teach Latin only because the Court required it. •

This method of school support prevailed until 1690. Its last years were marked by failure. Beginning in 1686, the school was maintained for but one half a year. From that time to 1690 the school was not maintained constantly, and the town was presented for failure to keep the school according to law. If we stop to inquire into the reasons for this, the only thing which appears on the records is a vote of 1683, that those dwelling on the west side of Stony Brook " should be freed from paying to the school in the year 1683 to the end they may be better able to teach their children amongst themselves."[1] This record indicates that the people living in the outer sections of Watertown were becoming conscious of the fact that they were not receiving their proportional benefit from the town school. If one section secured relief from paying the teachers, it follows that other groups felt an injustice in paying the rate. This naturally caused a disinclination to vote the rate, and hence the failure to maintain the school constantly during the years 1686 to 1690 and the consequent presentment to the Court. The failure of the old, and the necessity of the new method, of support was fully demonstrated. The town rate could no longer be levied for a central school.

The last decade of the century was the period of the combination of the town tax and the rate on scholars in the support of a central school. The town which had reached the highest point in the evolution of public school support had been compelled to regress. Under the proddings of the Court the town moved in 1690 to " keep " school " according to law."[2] In a later meeting of the same year it was " voted that the town will allow fifteen pounds towards a schoolmaster's maintenance provided that any of the inhabitants can agree with a person to keep the school so as to answer the law."[3] Evidently, the movement which appears in the minutes of the selectmen a few weeks later had already made some progress and was the occasion for this action. The sub-committee of the selectmen reported that they had agreed with Nathaniel Stone " to keep the school twenty

---

(1) Watertown Recs. II. p. 13.
(2) Ibid II. p. 39.
(3) Ibid II. p. 42.

II

persons having engaged to him to pay or see him paid ten pounds in money....and also the fifteen pounds granted by the town."[1] Without doubt most of these persons lived sufficiently close to the school for their children to get the benefit. This action represented the principle that payment should be made to the school in proportion to the benefit received. The town as a whole would vote fifteen pounds to avoid paying the fine of ten pounds but it would not stand more. The advantages enjoyed by the centre were in the estimation of its people sufficient to make the additional payment a just charge upon them.

This enunciation of the principle that the central school could not be supported wholly by a town rate received frequent repetition in the next few years. In 1693 the town still further limited the amount of the rate. The selectmen were instructed to get a master "provided they do not engage above five pounds in or as money." [2] The method adopted as a result was the regular combination of the town rate and tuition-tax. Mr. Norcross was again employed as the master to receive the five pounds from the town, three pence a week from reading, four pence from writing, and six pence from Latin, scholars. But even under these conditions there was opposition to the school. In 1696 the town refused to pay twenty pounds and then sent a committee " to pray the Court not to impose a fine on the town; and to inform the Court it is hopeful that the town will be provided with a school before the next quarter session."[3] On February first of the following year the town voted not to have a grammar school, but fearing the consequences, another town meeting, doubtless with other persons present, three weeks later rescinded the action, appropriated ten pounds from the town stock, and ordered " all scholars that are sent " to pay according to the studies pursued.[4] Mr. Goddard was again selected. Two years later he was elected in town meeting on the same terms to continue as long as he wished. It is not clear how long he remained, but it is plain that he did not receive part of the pay due him from the town.[5] As a result of his ceasing his labors the town found itself without a master in the year 1700 and with a fine imposed upon it by the Court of Quarter Sessions for its

(1) Watertown Recs. II. p. 43.
(2) Ibid II. p. 62.
(3) Ibid II. p. 108.
(4) Ibid II. p. 110.
(5) Ibid II. p. 139.

neglect.[1] The town proceeded in the same course the following year with Mr. Norcross again as master. But the town seems to have learned its lesson from this fine. The passage of the law of 1701 by the General Court, doubling the amount of the penalty, caused the inhabitants not to hesitate longer to make such an adjustment of their school administration as to secure them from future liability.

With 1701 begins the direct approach to the moving school. In the previous decade the unsatisfactory character of the standing school, even with the larger part of the salary paid by those whose children attended, was shown. A different adjustment in order to comply with the law was necessary. At this point there appears for the first time in school affairs the struggle that had been going on for some years between the different sections of the town in church affairs. This, no doubt, intensified the group feeling during the preceding decade and the disinclination of those at a distance from the school house to grant the school a large share of support by the town rate. In October 1701, five months after the passage of the provincial law, the agitation aroused by it was sufficient to cause the selectmen to call a town meeting to consider the question how " to build or procure a convenient place to keep a school in so that the inhabitants may be better accommodated to have their children taught to read and write. Also to take care to procure some meet person to keep a grammar school in said town as law requires, and to grant a salary for said service."[2] But the constable in the middle section of the town refused to warn the inhabitants and to return the order that he had so done.[3] The meeting was therefore compelled to adjourn without action. The reason for this, and also the bearing of the whole matter upon the question in hand, is shown in the difference between the first call of the selectmen and the second in the month following. They are of the same tenor throughout except that instead of stating " to build or procure a convenient *place* to keep a school in," it reads " to take care to build or procure a *place, or places.*"[4] This town meeting was accordingly held after warning in proper form and its action

---

[1] Watertown Recs. II. p. 132.
[2] Ibid II. p. 139.
[3] The part played by the westerly section, that which later became Weston, is uncertain.
[4] Watertown Recs. II. p. 140.

was that which we would be inclined to expect. It was then voted " that they will have a grammar school as the law requires: and said school to be kept the first quarter of the year at the old school house, and the second quarter of the year in the middle part of said town in such place as the town shall appoint: and the third quarter of the year at the old school house; and the fourth quarter of the year in such place in the middle part as the inhabitants of the town shall appoint."[1]   A rate of thirty pounds was also voted, the master to teach " the grammar as the law requires," reading, and writing. Those who sent their children in the winter season were required to bring a quarter of a cord of " good wood for their firing." [2]   There was no charge upon the scholars for the master's salary.

The uncertainty of being able to keep a master from year to year by a combination of the town rate and a charge on scholars had been fully proven. At the same time it was clearly evident that this was the only method by which the standing school could be maintained. The increased penalty of the law of 1701 made it prudent that something be done to better this precarious condition of affairs. But how was it to be done? The middle section of the town was clamoring for equal school advantages as well as equal church privileges, though perhaps not so vociferously. Yet their views in the solution of the question had to be reckoned with and their opposition appeased. They would not vote favors for the school in the eastern section even to save the town from a fine. They would support the school in an equal measure provided they got equal benefit. Consequently, they stood out for an equal share in the benefits of the school. When this was secured by a vote they were willing to vote for whatever was best for the school as a whole — that is the full support by town rate. Thus the law worked to compel the town rate. Division of the school was a prerequisite set up by those who did not fully share its benefits in order to secure their votes to the levy of the tax.

As in Malden both steps were taken at the same time. Their inseparable connection is clear. The entire support of the master by town rate and the moving school were preserved for many years thereafter.

---

[1] The west section of the town was excused from paying to the school on condition of paying the tax for the support of the ministry, and it was not considered in the apportionment of the school.   This was probably a permanent arrangement.
[2] Watertown Recs. II. pp. 140–1.

Having presented in detail the course of the movement in these two typical towns, it will be sufficient in discussing the other towns merely to show the connection between the abolition of the tuition-tax and the distribution of the school among the different sections. It is to be remembered in the consideration of these towns that the moving school was the result of the raising of the entire support by town rate because the outer sections would not vote for a large school rate unless they had some direct return from it in the form of a school supported wholly or partially by the proceeds of the tax, though they would usually vote for a small rate in order to save the town from the fine to which they would have to contribute.

In some of the towns which follow, the moving school was not formed at exactly the same time that the tuition-tax was abolished. Usually however it followed within a few years. As the dame school was a factor in the evolution of the moving school, the connection between school support and the moving school is to be traced in some instances through this institution. Then there were other towns whose first schools were supported entirely by the town rate; these invariably have the moving school or dame schools from almost the very beginning. These all illustrate and prove the principle, though in the latter class of towns the evolution cannot be shown because these schools were founded after entire support by rate became general. In the former class, on the other hand, progress was slower and another institution mediated in the working out of the movement. But in all cases in which there was entire support by town rate, distribution of the benefits of the town school in some form followed soon.

Manchester to 1724 supported its school entirely by tax on scholars.[1] Then tuition was abolished and the school was supported by the town rate entirely. But the amount given the master or dame to 1727 was but ten pounds, and in 1728 and 1729 but twenty pounds. The rate for the first years was not sufficient to stir up any opposition from the outer sections of the town, neither could the double amount in the latter period have produced much feeling. However, the appropriation in 1730 of forty-five pounds must have caused expression in no uncertain way of the demand from the outer sections for the benefit of the school. The next year it was cut to twenty pounds and the school was still maintained as a standing school. The record of

[1] Manchester Recs. I. pp. 70-155 passim.

1632 requires more extended attention,— " twenty-five pounds for the support of a free school." Four months later an appropriation of twenty-five pounds more was added " for the support of a free school or schools," and the committee chosen at the former meeting was instructed to dispose of the entire amount in the " hiring of a good and able schoolmaster." This indicates the first intention of the town to spend twenty-five pounds on a standing school in the centre of the town and a subsequent change to a moving school, with an expenditure of fifty pounds. However it is not called a moving school, and there is no mention of the places where it was kept. The reason for believing that it may have been such rests upon the fact that the phrase " school or schools " is used for the first of a number of times, in some of which it is certain that the outer sections had a town school. In the following year forty-five pounds was appropriated for the support of a " free school or schools " as before, showing the continuation of the same policy. No record of the action on schools in 1734 is extant. In 1735, the town was taxed fifty pounds " to support a free school in Manchester, the one-half of said fifty pounds to be expended to support four school dames ......[in sections of town specified]......and the other half ......to keep a free school in the school house in Manchester in the fall and winter seasons." In 1736 fifty pounds were again voted " for the support of a free school or schools " with the same distribution of the amount. In 1637 there was a great struggle between upholders of the central school and of the dame schools, in which the former won out by a vote of twenty-one to sixteen, and that year the " woman schools " were supported by a public subscription. The next year the moving master's school became a permanent institution in Manchester. From all this evidence it seems to be established that agitation for the benefit of the money paid in the school rate began as soon as the amount levied reached the point where it was regarded as considerable,— that is, definitely, by the year 1730. It is clear also that this sentiment produced visible results in the records within two years thereafter which led to the establishment of the moving school, either immediately or eight years later through the mediation of the dame school during the intervening years.[1]

---

[1] Manchester Recs. I. pp. 154, 163, 166, 170, 173, 175, 180, 182, 184, 187, 191, 198; II. pp. 22, 23, 26, et seq.

To 1687, except in the earliest years, Newbury supported its central school by a combination of the two methods. In that years it was continued, but five pounds was given to each of the two " ends " of the town to support a school. At the same time the amount to be expended for the master was reduced by ten pounds. In 1689 the appropriation for the " ends " was omitted; the centre received twenty pounds, and the scholars paid as in 1687. In 1690, the amount was raised to twenty-five pounds. Apparently, the last amount was a little too large to please those living at a distance from the school. So in the year following the amount was increased to that of 1687, and the school made a moving school free of charge to " readers," the " ends " getting their return from the tax in this manner instead of in a direct return of the money as in that year. The connection between an increase in the appropriation for schools above a certain amount and the demand of the outer sections for a participation in its benefit seems clear. This principle was counterbalanced by other considerations, however, and the moving school was discontinued at the end of the year. The tuition system had not lost its hold upon the people, and the town employed a master who was also to assist the pastor of the church. From that time the town history says nothing of the schools during a period of ten years. Then its tuition-tax had been displaced, and the school was a divided school. The development during these years could not be followed in this study even if it were desirable. There is no doubt, nevertheless, that the principle set forth in this chapter prevailed in this town.[1]

Worcester probably supported its first school in 1726 by a town rate. It was a standing school until 1731. During these five years there were evidently differences of opinion expressed upon two points concerning them. The first was whether they should have a school at all. This appears in the December meeting of 1726 and the May meeting of 1727. Whether any of the opposition to the school had a basis in the fact that it was a standing school cannot be asserted positively, but it is reasonable to expect that this was responsible in some measure. The second point was concerning the location of the school. The settling of this question was referred in 1730 to a committee of five men. There is no doubt this difficulty arose over the fact

---

[1] Currier, Newbury, pp. 396-401.

that the school was a standing school, and that all desired to have it as near to their homes as possible.   Six months later in the April meeting this sentiment realized itself in definite provision for dame schools at the charge of the town for the summer ; and in the next September the master's school was made a moving school.   It was from that time a permanent institution until it gave way to the divided school.   The amounts of money expended on schools was after this time about double what it had been previously.   The inseparable connection between the town rate and the moving school seems clear, though the one was not realized until a few years after the other.[1]

In Deerfield the school from 1698 to 1722 was supported by a combined tax on scholars and estates, the amount of the town rate varying from fifteen pounds to twenty pounds.   In the latter year the children were required to furnish only firewood.   The standing school supported by town rate remained the only town school for six years, the amount of the master's wages for one year being thirty-five pounds.   The first indication given of group consciousness among the outer sections in school matters occurred in 1728 when liberty was given " to farmers to procure school dames to teach their children."   This custom prevailed in the town proper until the sections became definitely marked and the divided school was evolved.   However in 1740 the town school became a moving school going into two places in the town.[2]

The towns which did not have any school until the early part of the eighteenth century supported them from the beginning by town rate.   All of them recognized the claim of the different sections of the town for the school from the first.   Thus Duxbury in 1709, Sutton in 1730, Tisbury in 1737, Weston in 1754, and Fitchburg in 1764 had moving schools as their first town schools of which there is record.   Brookline had as its first town schools two dame schools in summer and a moving masters' school in winter.[3]   Lunenburg, the first year (1732) had four masters' schools ; in 1734, four dames ; and in 1737 the moving school.   Altho Grafton's first school in 1736 was a standing school, the following year it was made a moving school.   Amherst's first schools were dame schools, which later developed into the divided school.

[1] Worcester Recs. 1879, II. pp. 39, 47, 48, 49, 53, 59, 62, 66, 70, 73, et seq.
[2] Sheldon, Deerfield I. pp. 273-4, 570; II. pp. 839-40.   The history of Deerfield which is unusually full and accurate on school affairs does not give sufficient material for us to trace out with entire satisfaction this particular movement.
[3] As a "hamlet" of Boston it had had previously two standing schools.

Dudley's first school in 1739 was, on the other hand, a divided school. So was the first school in the records of Lancaster. In Oxford the voting of the first school rate in 1734 carried with it the establishment of the moving school, though they probably had had a town schoolmaster for years previous. While these cases do not show the evolution of the moving school, they serve to establish the universality of the principle that total support of the school by town rate carried with it a distribution of the school to all in as equal manner as possible.[1]

In some towns this recognition of the rights of the outer sections to the town school took on the form of separate or divided schools. The principle of connection between the change in support and in the character of the school applies equally well to both the divided or moving school, for both were a recognition of the rights of the outer sections and the particular form the school took was a subsidiary matter. Those towns in which the divided school was formed from the central town school may be examined therefore as offering confirmatory evidence of the validity of the principle under discussion. These may be noted only briefly, however.

Plymouth [2] is one of the best examples to show the close relationship between support and form of school. The school, when it was maintained, was up to 1696, a standing school. Tuition was the method used certainly to 1693, either in whole or in part, and possibly to 1696. In that year the master was paid thirty-three pounds, raised by rate, and the school was a moving school into four places. The next record of the school in 1699 shows it to be a central school with the combination of the town rate and tuition-rate. Although in 1700 the town ordered a school, there seems to have been none held for the town was presented in the following year. The school in 1703 was evidently a central school supported by the combined methods. In 1704 occurred the only exception to the general rule — a central grammar school supported wholly by taxation. Most probably that method was resorted to by reason of the

(1) Duxbury Recs., p. 208; Tisbury Recs., p. 101; Weston Recs., p. 29; Brookline Recs., p. 96; Benedict and Tracy, Sutton, p. 499; Fitchburg Recs. I. p. 7; Lunenburg Recs., pp. 70, 94. 99; Pierce, Grafton, p. 259; Amherst Recs., p. 18; Dudley Recs., p. 76; Lancaster Recs., p, 189; Daniels, Oxford, p. 96.
(2) It is interesting to observe in some of the cases, as Plymouth and Braintree, how the moving and divided school were both used.

fear of the fine; it was the only method by which the town could then furnish a school. The opposition of the outer sections is evidenced in the act of the town for the following year. It was then arranged that the town should give twenty pounds a year for seven years and that " sundry inhabitants," presumably in the centre, should provide and administer a school in the centre of the town. All scholars not children of the subscribers were required to pay tuition in the town according to distance from the school. In 1712 this arrangement was extended for four years. In 1716 entire town support was readopted and three schools were established for the term of five years. In 1722 the grammar school was made a " movable " school in three places. The central town school was no more. With the exception of a single year in all these kaleidoscopic changes, entire support by town rate and a divided or moving school occurred together; on the other hand, the combined method of support and the central school occurred together.[1]

In Braintree " quarter money " was in all probability paid until 1703. The next record concerning the school is in the year 1715, by which time it had disappeared. The next year the school was made a divided school, one school being held in the North Parish, another in the South. In 1719 the school in the South Parish was made a moving school; and in 1721 there was an unsuccessful attempt to have the grammar school made a moving school between the two parishes.[2]

The schools in Salem were supported entirely by gifts, income from funds, and tuition to 1734. Before 1700 the outer sections demanded a share from the proceeds of the school fund. They obtained it with a fair degree of regularity from 1700 to 1734. These outer sections spent the money as they saw fit, part of the time having a moving school. The desire to levy money for the support of this school was alleged by " the village " as a reason for separation from Salem proper. This agitation finally led to the town levying a tax for schools. The return from the first school tax was returned to the various sections that had paid it. Thus the rights of the outlying population were fully recognized.[3]

[1] Plymouth Recs. I. pp. 122, 224, |245, 246, 270, 276, 289, 303, 316, 319; II. pp. 1, 5, 8, 21, 42, 72, 94, 97, 169, 217.
[2] Braintree Recs., pp. 2, 18, 47, 54, 86, 88, 98, 103.
[3] Felt. Salem I. pp. 427-447.

Springfield never had a moving school. It is different from the towns thus far presented in another point as well, and this point is of considerable importance in this connection. Although recognition of the rights of all the sections to a share of the town rate did not come until after the school was supported wholly by that means, yet one or two of the most populous were put on almost equal terms with the village proper before that time. Furthermore, Springfield presents a long account of great interest which cannot be entered upon here. The bitterness of the struggle and the appeals of the town first to the Court of Quarter Sessions and later to the General Court itself for a decision upon the question of the legal means of school support are the principal features. It seems to have been a question whether the combined method or the town rate alone was the correct one. Finally, after the final appeal to the General Court in 1713 the town rate seems to have been permanently adopted. Division of the town into six precincts came three years later, each precinct receiving back all the money its inhabitants paid in the school rate. The close relationship between the two acts is plain.[1]

There were some towns which had a moving school before the abolition of the tax on scholars. Medford furnishes an example of this class. In 1719 its first school was supported by tuition alone. In 1720 the town voted an eight pound tax " for ye support and encouragement of ye school ye ensuing winter in each part of ye town namely ye east and west sides of said town." It seems that the raising of any amount at all by rate was a sufficient cause in the minds of the inhabitants of this town to demand the fullest possible participation in the benefit of the school.[2] The number of towns which divided or moved the school before tuition was abolished must have been very few, however, as compared with the number of towns which did not. Springfield and Medford are the only cases found by the author.

It remains now to notice those towns in which a long period of time intervened between the time of the abolition of the tax on scholars and the distribution of the school among the various parts of the town. Those towns which had a compact popula-

---

(1) Burt, Springfield I. pp. 131, 137; II. pp. 137, 173, 372-3, 375, 380, 382-3, 315, 387, 391-2, 396, 399.
(2) Morss, The Development of the Public School of Medford. Medford Historical Register III. pp. 4-6, 20.

tion would not feel this tendency. Northampton, located on the frontier, because of Indian troubles, was compelled to have its dwellings near each other. Just as soon as this danger was removed the population began to extend to the outer parts of the town. Thus in Northampton the school became free from tuition charges in 1692; population began to spread in 1730 and 1731; and schools were established in the outer parts in 1743, when a new precinct was established.[1]

Dedham is another town in which the abolition of the tax on scholars seems to have had no appreciable effect on the creation of the moving school. From 1694 the school was supported entirely by the town rate, but the moving school was not established until 1717.[2] Mr. Slafter in his study of the " Schools and Schoolmasters of Dedham " offers no explanation of the creation of the moving school.[3] The author of this study is at a loss to estimate with any degree of confidence the weight of the various factors in producing the result. There are no other towns, however, whose records extend down to the time of the beginning of the moving school, or whose histories present sufficient material for a basis of judgment, in so far as the author has been able to examine them, which do not show clearly the working of this principle of a fair return from the school to all sections so soon as it became supported entirely by town rate. The above evidence establishes inseparable connection between the abolition of the tuition-tax and the establishment of the moving school in a number of towns, and the strong influence of the former act in providing the later in many more. Furthermore, it is clear that it produced the divided school in those towns where the moving school does not appear in the evolution of the school district. On the other hand, there is nothing in the history of those few in which no connection is apparent to disprove the general principle.

The abandonment of the tuition-tax is, therefore, presented as one of the causes, and as the most immediate cause, of the creation of the moving school.

---

[1] Trumbull, Northampton I. p. 426; II. pp. 15-32, 38.
[2] Dedham Recs. V. p. 229.
[3] Slafter, p. 45.

CONCLUSION

As a result of this study it is clear that in the evolution of school control and school support each town proceeded in its own way, influenced comparatively little by the practices of other towns, and that the great steps in advance were caused by the legislation of the General Court. This legislation did not, however, affect the movement directly, but indirectly, through the setting up of standards which it required the towns to reach, or through the general spirit which it expressed and which the towns endeavored to realize. The General Court acted, on the other hand, only when the measures used by the towns failed to bring the desired results. Thus the evolution really took place in the towns, with the General Court as the superior body compelling the advance which brought about in the towns the abandonment of the old and the establishment of the new. The movement in school control was from aristocratic to democratic control, in school support it was from free contribution, through the compulsory contribution and the combination of the town rate and the tuition-tax, to the town rate alone.

The changes in society which made the old central school unsatisfactory were due to the decline of the dominance of the religious motives and the gradual introduction and growth of economic interests. This gradual transition produced new wants. One of these was the desire to live upon the farming land. Thus the original compact village of dwelling houses became dispersed. The industry of agriculture in dispersed settlements together with the decline of the religious motives for education greatly lowered the interest in schools, so that the people became content with short terms of instruction and meagre attainments. The same change in the motives of life also affected the political development. Aristocratic tendencies largely disappeared and pure democracy prevailed. The private schools furnished to those in the outskirts of the town the rudiments of instruction for as long a time as the children could well attend and at no greater, and possibly at a less, cost than what the parents would have to pay at the more distant town school. In consequence, it became more and more difficult to get a town rate voted, and a sufficient number of children to come to school to afford proper return from the tuition-tax. The neighborhood and parish jealousies and quarrels contributed also to this end.

Finally, it came to the point where schools were not being maintained at all in some towns, and but for a part of the year in many more. In this emergency the General Court stepped in, and for the welfare of the state increased the amount of the fine to be imposed on the towns for non-observance of the law, and caused a more rigorous enforcement of the new than of the old law. The towns preferred to spend their money raised by rate for a school than to turn it over as a fine to the neighboring town or towns which obeyed the law for the benefit of their schools. But those living at a distance from the centre refused to vote the town rate as the means of sole support for the school unless they could have more direct benefit from the school. The people of the centre who had been getting most benefit from the school were then compelled to yield to the demands of the outer sections and to grant the moving of the school into the outlying portions of the town,—thus creating the moving school.

This completes the presentation of the first step in the process of the development of the school district in Massachusetts. In general, the date for the completion of this step may be placed in the first quarter of the eighteenth century. The next major division in that development may be placed at the year 1789 when the school district was recognized by state law. From that time to 1827 was the period of the perfection of the school district. The steps in this latter period may be traced in a general way by the state laws. The middle portion of the entire development, that of the establishment of the school district, from 1725 to 1789, is not so plain. Inasmuch as the author has gathered much of the material for this period, he offers here the outline of that development as it appears to him.

Account must be taken of four separate and distinct, yet related, sub-movements. Each town proceeded in its own way as before. Some progressed rapidly along one line, other towns along another line. Still other towns were backward along the same lines in which these towns had attained considerable development. The rate of progress, moreover, was not uniform; often, also, there was retrogression.

These sub-movements and the steps in each from the moving school to the establishment of the school district were as follows:

(1) Toward definite bounds.
> (a) Number and location of places for moving school changed from year to year.
> (b) School houses built and thus centres established.
> (c) Bounds between sections defined.

(2) Toward one teacher for each section—from school to schools.
> (a) One teacher for the entire town.
> (b) One for part of the whole number of places or sections.
> (c) One for each section.

(3) Toward maximum benefit from school tax.
> (a) Length of time school kept in each place fixed arbitrarily.
> (b) School kept in each section according to amount of school tax paid by parents of children who attend them.
> (c) Each section receives back from the town all the money paid in for schools by its inhabitants.

(4) Toward most direct control by sections.
> (a) Town meeting, the legislative organ; the selectmen, the ministerial organ.
> (b) Town meeting, the legislative organ; the school committee, the ministerial organ, chosen without reference to number or location of school or schools.
> (c) Town meeting, the legislative organ; the school committee, the ministerial organ, one member chosen from each section as its representative.

APPENDIX A

BOSTON

From Second Report of the Record Commissioners. Boston 1881.

13 Apr. 1635 — Likewise it was then generally agreed upon, that our brother Philemon Pormont, shalbe intreated to become scholemaster, for the teaching and nourtering of children with us.

p. 5.

The last record in the original first volume of town records is written on page 161. On page 162 are written two memoranda; page 163 is blank; page 164 contains further memoranda. On page 165 is the record here given.

" 12th of the 6th, August, 1636.

At a general meeting of the richer inhabitants there was given towards the maintenance of a free school master for the youth with us, Mr. Daniel Maud being now also chosen thereunto: —

The Governor, Mr. Henry Vane, Esq., x l.
The Deputy Governor, Mr. John Winthrop, Esq., x l.

Mr. Richard Bellingham, xl s.	William Hudson, ———.
Mr. Wm. Coddington, xxx s.	William Pierce, xx s.
Mr. Winthrop, Jr., xx s.	John Audley, iiii s.
Mr. Wm. Hutchinson, xx s.	John Button, vi s.
Mr. Robte. Keayne, xx s.	Edward Bendall, v s.
Thomas Leveritt, x s.	Isaac Grosse, v s.
William Coulbourn, viii s.	Zakye Bosworth, iiii s.
John Coggeshall, xiii s. iiii d.	William Salter, iiii s.
John Coggan, xx s.	James pennyman, v s.
Robte. Harding, xiii s. iiii d.	John Pemberton, iii s.
John Newgate, x s.	John Bigges, iiii s.
Richard Tuttell, x s.	Sameull Wilkes, x s.
Wm. Aspenall, viii s.	Mr. Cotton, ———.
John Sampford, viii s.	Mr. Wilson, xx s.
Samuel Cole, x s.	Richard Wright, vi s. viii d.
William Balstone, vi s. 8 d.	Thomas Marshall, vi s. 8 d.
William Brenton,———.	William Talmage, iiii s.
James Penne, vi s. 8 d.	Richard Gridley, iiii s.
Jacob Ellyott, vi s. 8 d.	Thomas Savidge, v s.
Nicholas Willys, ———.	Edward Ransforde, v s.
Raphe Hudson, x s.	Edward Hutchinson, iiii s.

p. 160 Note.

11 Jan. 1642 — at a general Townsmeeting — " Its Ordered that Deare-Island shall be Improoved for the maintennance of a free schoole for the Towne, and such other Occasions as the Townsmen For the time being shall thinke meet, the sayd schoole being sufficiently Provided for." p. 65.

2 Jan 1645 — at a meeting of the selectmen — " Its ordered that the Constables shall pay unto Deacon Eliot for the use of mr Woodbridge eight pounds due to him for keeping the Schoole the Last yeare. p. 82.

30 Jan. 1645 — at a meeting of the selectmen — " Deare Island is let to hire unto James Penn, and John Oliver for these three years next ensuing paying unto the Use of the Schoole seaven pounds per yeare." p. 82.

The following extract from Winthrop's History of New England, written by him in 1645 (month and day uncertain), throws a flood of light upon the method of supporting the school in Boston. Although it is not an official record, it is because of its importance given a place here.

" Divers free schools were created as at Roxbury — and at Boston (where they made an order to allow fifty pounds to the master and an house and thirty pounds to an usher, who should also teach to read and write and cipher, and Indians children were to be taught freely, and the charge to be yearly by contribution, either by voluntary allowance, or by rate of such as refused, etc., and this order was confirmed by the General Court ———). Other towns did the like providing maintenance by several means." Savage (new edition), II. 264.

CHARLESTOWN

From Frothingham's History of Charlestown, Boston, 1845.

3 June 1636 — " Mr William Witherall was agreed with to keep a school for a twelve month to begin the eighth of August and to have four pounds this year " p. 65.

20 Jan. 1647 — " It was agreed that a rate of fifteen pounds should be gathered of the town, towards the school for this year, and the five pounds that Major Sedgwick is to pay this year (for the island) for the school, also the town part of Mistick wear for the school forever " In the margin " allowance granted for the school." p. 115.

Regarding that part of the so-called records previous to 1662 from which the above are taken the author says: — " Its traditionary character appears upon its face. It certainly cannot be relied on as to dates. Nor can the remainder of the volume be depended upon as an exact transcript of the original."

12

DEDHAM

From Vol. III of Dedham Records, (Dedham 1892)

2 Jan. 1643 " Also it was with an vnanimous consent concluded that some portion of land in this entended deuision should be set a part for publique vse: viz for the Town the Church & A fre Schoole viz: 40 acres at the least or 60 acres at the most."

p. 92.

1 Jan. 1645 — " The sd Inhabitants takeing into Consideration the great necesitie of prouiding some means for the Education of the youth in or sd Town did with an vnanimous consent declare by voate their willingness to promote that worke promising to put too their hands to prouide maintenance for a Free Schoole in our said Towne.

And farther did risolue & consent testefying it by voate to rayse the some of Twenty pounds p annu: towards the maintaining of a Schoole mr to keep a free Schoole in our sd Towne

And also did resolue & consent to betrust the sd 20£ p annu: & certaine lands in or Towne formerly set a part for publique vse: into the hand of Feofees to be presently Chosen by themselues to imploy the sd 20£ and the land aforesd to be improued for the vse of the said Schoole: that as the profits shall arise from ye sd land euery man may be proportionably abated of his some of the sd 20£ aforesaid freely to be giuen to ye vse aforesaid. And yt ye said Feofees shall haue power to make a Rate for the necesary charg of improuing the sd land: they giueing account thereof to the Towne or to those whome they should depute "

p. 105.

4 Jan. 1645 — " Granted to the Feosees for ye free Schoole in Dedham for the vse of the sd Schoole a percell of the Training ground so much as shalbe set out to them by the Towne which said pcell is granted from this present day vnto the last day of the Eight month which shalbe in ye yeare 1650

Hen: Chickeringe Eli Lusher & Hen Phillips deputed to set out the sd parcell of land aboue said "

p. 108

DORCHESTER

From Fourth Report of the Record Commissioners of Boston (1880)

" It is ordered that the 20th of May 1639, that there shalbe a rent of 20£ yeerely foreur imposed vpon Tomsons Iland to bee payd p euy p'son that hath p'rtie in the said Iland according to the p'portion that any such p'son shall fro tyme to tyme injoy and posesse there, and this towards the mayntenance of a schoole in Dorchestr this rent of 20£ yeerely to bee payd to such a schoolemaster as shall undertake to teach english latin and othe tongues, and also writing the sayd schoolmaster to bee chosen fro tyme p the freemen and that is left to the discresion of elders and the 7 men for the tyme beeing whether maydes shalbe taught with the boyes or not. For the levying this 20£ yeerely fro the p'ticuler p'sons that ought to pay that according to this order. It is farther ordered that somme man shalbe apoynted p the 7 men for the tyme beeing to Receiue that and refusall to levye that p distresse, and not fynding distresse such p'son as so refuseth payment shall forfeit the land he hath in p'prietie in the sayd Island." p. 39.

31 Oct. 1639 — " It is ordered that Mr. Waterhouse shall be dispence'd with concerneing that Clause of the order in the Charge of Twenty pounds yeerely, rent to be payd for Tomsons Iland towards the skool: where he is bound to teach to write it shalbe left to his liberty in that poynt of teaching to write, only to doe what he can conviently therein." p. 40.

1 Feb. 1641.— " The same day the Elders Mr. Stoughton and Mr. Glouer are intrusted p the towne to sett Tomsons Iland att a Rent for the best Benefitt of the schoole." p. 44.

7 Mar 1642.— " Wheras the Inhabitants of Dorchester haue formerly ordered Consented and agreed that a Rate of Twentie pound p ann shall issue and be payd by the sayd Inhabitants and there heires from and out of a Certaine porcon of land in Dorchester Called Tomsons Iland for and towards the maintenance of a schoole in Dorchester aforsayd. And that uppon experience it is found to be a matter of great labour and difficultie to collect the sayd rent from soe many seuerall p'sons as ought to paye the same accordinge there seuerall p'portions the p'sones that haue title to land in the sayd Iland and who therefore ought to pay the sayd rent, beinge noe lesse in number than Twentie pound when it is duly collected and payd is not of it selfe suffitient maintenance, for a schoole without some addicon therunto for the augmentinge therfor of the sayd rent and to the intent that the same may henceforth be more readily collected and payd It is heerby ordered and all the pesent Inhabitants of dorchester aforsayd Whose names are heervnto subscribed doe for themselues and there heires heerby Couenant consent and aggree that from henceforth the said Iland and all the benefitt and prfitts therof and all there right and Interest in the same shallbe wholy and for euer bequeathed and given away from themselues and their heires vnto the Towne of Dorchester aforesayd for and Towards the maintenance of a free schoole in Dorchester aforsaid for the instructinge and Teching of Children and youth in good literature and Learninge. And to the intent that the better maintenance for a free schoole as is heerby intended may arise from and out of the sayd Iland It is therefore the mynd of the prsent

donoures that the sayd Iland shall from tyme to tyme be lett, assigned and set ouer by the Inhabitants of Dorchester for the time beinge or theire agents for such yearlie rent or rents as shall in Common Estimation amount to the full value of the sayd Iland."

Memorand. that before the subscribinge of these prsents the donoures aforsayd did further agree and declare that it was and is there mynd and true intencons that if at any tyme ther shall happen and fall out a vacancie and want of a schoolmaster by means of death or otherwise, yet the rents and prfitts ishuinge and arisinge of the sayd Iland shalbe converted and applied only to and for the maintenance and vse of the schoole either by augmentinge the stipend for a schoolemaster or otherwise but not for any other vse."   pp. 104-5.

Upon a generall and lawfull warning of all the Inhabitants the 14th of the 1st moneth 1645 these rules and orders prsented to the Towne concerning the Schoole of Dorchester are Confirmed by the maior p'te of the Inhabitants then pesent.

First It is ordered that three able, and sufficient men of the Plantation shalbe Chosen to bee wardens or ouseers of the Schoole aboue mentioned who shall haue the charge ousight and ordering therof and of all things concerning the same in such manner as is hereafter expressed and shall Continue in their office and place for terme of their liues respectiuely, vnlesse by reason of any of them Remouing his habitation out of the Towne, or for any other weightie reason the Inhabitants shall see cause to Elect or Chuse others in their roome in which cases and vpon the death of any of the sayd wardens the Inhabitants shall make a new Election and choice of others.

And Mr. Haward, Deacon Wiswall, Mr. Atherton are elected to bee the first wardens or ouseers.

Secondly, the said Wardens shall haue full power to dispose of the Schoole stock whither the same bee in land or otherwyse, both such as is already in beeing and such as may by any good meanes heereafter bee added: and shall Collect and receiue the Rents, Issues and p'fitts arising and growing of and from the sayd stock, And the sayd rents Issues and b'fits shall imploy and lay out only for the best behoof, and advantadge of the sayd Schoole; and the furtherance of learning thereby, and shall giue a faythfull and true accoumpt of there receipts and disbursements so often as they shalbe thervnto required by the Inhabitants or the maior p'te of them.

Thirdly the said Wardens shall take care, and doe there vtmost and best endeavor that the sayd Schoole may fro tyme to tyme bee supplied with an able and sufficient Schoolemaster who neuthelesse is not to be admitted into the place of Schoolemaster without the Generall cosent of the Inhabitants or the maior p'te of them.

Fowerthly so often as the sayd Schoole shalbe supplied with a Schoolemr — so p'vided and and admitted, as aforsayd the wardens shall fro tyme to tyme pay or cause to be payd vnto the sayd Schoolemaster such wages out of the Rents, Issues and p'fitts of the Schoole stocke as shall of right come due to be payd.

Fiuethly the sayd wardens shall from tyme to tyme see that the Schoole howse bee kept in good, and sufficient repayre, the chargs of which reparacion shalbe defrayed and payd out of such Rents, Issues and p'fitts of the Schoole stock, if there be sufficient, or elese of such rents as shall arise and grow in the time of the vacancy of the schoolemr — if there bee any such and in defect of such vacancy the wardens shall repayre to the 7 men of the Towne for the tyme beeing who shall haue power to taxe the Towne with such some, or sommes as shalbe requisite for the repayring of the Schoole howse as aforsayd..........
....

5ly hee shall equally and impartially receiue, and instruct such as shalbe sent and Comitted to him for that end whither their parents bee poore or rich not refusing any who haue Right and Interest in the Schoole.   pp. 54-5.

NEWBURY

From Currier's History of Newbury (Boston, 1902).

" There was granted unto Anthony Somerby in the year 1639 for his incouragement to keepe schoole for one yeare foure Akers of upland over the great river in the necka, also sixe Akers of salt marsh next to Abraham Toppan's twenty akers, the which twenty Akers lyes on the south side of it."   p. 395.

SALEM

From Essex Institute Historical Collections, v. IX (Salem, 1869).

" Att a generall Towne meeting in le 11th month 1639
Voted — Yong Mr. Norris Chose by this assemblie to teach skoole "   p. 97.

" At a generall towne meeting held the 35th of the 7th moneth 1644.

Ordered that a note be published one the next Lecture day that such as have children to be kept at schoole would bring in their names & what they will give for one whole year & Also That if any poore body hath children or a childe to be put to school & not able to pay for their schooling That the Towne will pay it by rate."   p. 132.

IPSWICH

From Felt's History of Ipswich, Essex and Hamilton (Cambridge, 1834).

" 1636 A grammer school is set up, but does not succeed p.83 "[1]

1642 "The town votes that there shall be a free school " p.87

---

[1] Felt says of this entry: "a note, though it has the appearance of being copied. "

APPENDIX B

The following is a portion of the Agreement entered into by the inhabitants of Roxbury in the "last of August 1645" at the time of the establishment of "The Free School of 1645 in Roxburie" (From Dillaway's A History of the Grammar School, Roxbury, 1860).

"Whereas, the Inhabitantes of Roxburie, in consideration of their relligeous care of posteritie, have taken into consideration how necessarie the education of theire children in Literature will be to fitt them for public service, both in Churche and Commonwealthe, in succeeding ages. They therefore unanimously have consented and agreed to erect a free schoole in the said Towne of Roxburie, and to allow Twenty pounds per annum to the Schoolemaster, to bee raised out of the Messuages and part of the Lands of the severall donors (Inhabitants of the said Towne) in severall proportions as hereafter followeth under theire handes.

(1645) "In consideration of the premises, the Donors hereafter expressed for the severall proportions or annuities by them voluntarily undertaken and underwritten, Have given and granted and by these presents doe for themselves their heires and Asignees respectively hereby give and grant unto the present Feoffees, ...
....
the severall rents and summes hereafter expressed under their handes issueing and going forth of their severall messuages lands and tenements, in Roxburie hereafter expressed. To have and to hould receive and enjoy the said annual rents or summes to the only use of the Free School in Roxburie, yearly payable at or upon the last of September by even portions: the first portion to begin the last of September this present yeare."

The author gives six men, as each pledging his dwelling house. He then states,—" In like manner other names, houses or lands, with the yearly donations against the names. But it is not necessary to insert the whole. The names and sums only will be copied." There were sixty-four donors, pledging in all over twenty-one pounds a year, the individual subscription ranging from one pound, four shillings to two shillings.

The following year it was agreed " by all those of the inhabitants of Roxbury as have or shall subscribe their names or marks to this book for themselves severally and for their respective heirs and executors, that not only their houses, but their fields, orchards, gardens, outhouses and homesteads shall be and hereby are bound and made liable to and for the several sums and rents before and hereafter in this book mentioned to be paid by every of them. Dated this XXVIII of December 1646." But only twelve names are affixed.

LIST OF REFERENCES

Histories and Historical Essays—General.

EGGLESTON, EDWARD. The Transit of Civilization. New York, 1901.
GNEIST, RUDOLPH. The History of the English Constitution, translated by Philip A. Ashworth. New York, 1886. 2 v.
GOODNOW, FRANK JOHNSON. Politics and Administration. New York, 1900.
HOWARD, GEORGE ELLIOTT. An Introduction to the Local Constitutional History of the United States, in Johns Hopkins University Studies in Historical and Political Science, extra v. 4. Baltimore, 1889.
NICHOLS, SIR GEORGE. A History of the English Poor Law, edited by H. S. Willink. New York, 1898. 2 v.
DOYLE, JOHN ANDREW. English Colonies in America. New York, 1882-1907. 5 v.
OSGOOD, HERBERT L. The American Colonies in the Seventeenth Century. New York, 1904, 1907. 3 v.

Histories and Historical Essays—New England and Massachusetts.

ADAMS, BROOKS. The Emancipation of Massachusetts. Boston, 1887.
ADAMS, CHARLES FRANCIS. Three Episodes of Massachusetts History. Boston, 1896. 2 v.
ADAMS, HENRY BAXTER. Germanic Origin of New England Towns, in Johns Hopkins University Studies in Historical and Political Science, v. 1, No. 2. Baltimore, 1882.
DOUGLAS, CHARLES H. J. Financial History of Massachusetts from the organization of the Massachusetts Bay Colony to the American Revolution, in Columbia University Studies in History, Economics, and Public Law, v. 1, No. 4. New York, 1892.
HUTCHINSON, THOMAS. The History of Massachusetts from the first settlement thereof in 1628 until the year 1750. Boston, 1795. 2 v.
PALFREY, JOHN GORHAM. History of New England. Boston, 1883-1894. 5 v.
WEEDEN, WILLIAM B. Economic and Social History of New England, 1620-1789. Boston, 1894. 2 v.
WHITTEN, ROBERT HARVEY. Public Administration of Massachusetts; the Relation of Central to Local Activity, in Columbia University Studies in History, Economics, and Public Law. New York, 1898.
WINTHROP, JOHN. The History of New England from 1630 to 1649, second edition, edited by James Savage. Boston, 1853.

Church Histories.

BACKUS, ISAAC. A History of New England with particular reference to the denomination of Christians called Baptists, second edition. Newton, Massachusetts, 1871. 2 v.

DEXTER, HENRY MARTIN. The Congregationalism of the last Three Hundred Years as Seen in its Literature. New York, 1886.

FELT, JOSEPH B. The Ecclesiastical History of New England. Boston, 1855, 1862. 2 v.

TIFFANY, CHARLES C. A History of the Protestant Episcopal Church in the United States of America. New York, 1895.

UHDEN, HERMAN FERDINAND. The New England Theocracy; a history of the Congregationalists in New England to revivals of 1740, translated from second German edition by H. C. Conant. Boston, 1859.

WALKER, WILLISTON. History of the Congregational Churches in the United States. New York, 1894. 2 v.

Histories of Education.

BROWN, ELMER ELLSWORTH. The Making of Our Middle Schools. New York, 1903.

BUSH, GEORGE GARY. The First Common Schools of New England, in report of Commissioner of Education of the United States, 1896-1897, pp. 1165-1186.

CLEWS, ELSIE M. Educational Legislation and Administration of the Colonial Governments, in Columbia University Contribution to Philosophy, Psychology and Education. New York, 1899.

DEXTER, EDWIN GRANT. A History of Education in the United States. New York, 1904.

DILLAWAY, C. K. A History of the Grammar School or "The Free Schools of 1645 in Roxburie." Roxbury, 1860.

GRANT, JAMES M. A. History of the Burgh Schools of Scotland. London, 1876.

JOHNSON, CLIFTON. The Country School in New England. New York, 1893.

MARTIN, GEORGE H. The Evolution of the Massachusetts Public School System. New York, 1894.

MONROE, PAUL. History of Education. New York, 1905.

DE MONTMORENCY, J. E. G. The Progress of Education in England; a sketch of the development of English educational organizations from early times to the year 1904. London, 1904.

DE MONTMORENCY, J. E. G. State Intervention in English Education; a short history from the earliest times. Cambridge, 1902.

MORSS, C. H. The Development of the Public School of Medford, in Medford Historical Register, III, pp. 1-41.

SLAFTER, CARLOS. The Schools and Teachers of Dedham, Massachusetts, 1644-1904. Deadham, 1905.

STOWE, A. MONROE. English Grammar Schools in the Reign of Queen Elizabeth in Teachers College Contributions to Education. *In preparation.*

SUZZALO, HENRY. The Rise of Local School Supervision in Massachusetts, in Teachers College Contributions to Education. New York, 1906.

Laws.

The Colonial Laws of Massachusetts, reprinted from the edition of 1660 with the supplements to 1672, containing also the Body of Liberties 1641, edited by William H. Whitmore. Boston, 1889.

Records of the Governor and Company of the Massachusetts Bay, edited by Nathaniel Bradstreet Shurtleff. Boston, 1853-1854. 5 v.

Acts and Resolves of the Province of the Massachusetts Bay. Boston, 1869-1881.

Local Histories.

Andover, Historical Sketches of. SARAH LOVING BAILEY. Boston, 1880.

Billerica, History of. HENRY A. HAZEN. Boston, 1883.

Cambridge, History of. LUCIEN R. PAIGE. Boston, 1877.

Charleston, The History of. RICHARD FROTHINGHAM. Boston, 1845.

Concord in the Colonial Period, being a history of the town of. CHARLES H. WALCOTT. Boston, 1884.

Dedham, History of. ERASTUS WORTHINGTON. Boston, 1827.

Deerfield, Massachusetts, A History of. GEORGE SHELDON. Deerfield, 1896.

Essex County, Standard History of. C. W. F. ARCHER, ELIAS MASON, and others. Boston, 1878.

Fitchburg, Massachusetts, History of the town of, comprising also a history of Lunenberg from its first settlement to the year 1764. Fitchburg, 1865.

Hadley, History of. SYLVESTER JUDD. Northampton, 1865.

Haverhill, History of. GEORGE WINGATE CHASE. Haverhill, 1861.

Ipswich, History of, Essex, and Hamilton, Cambridge, 1834.

Lancaster, Massachusetts, History of, from the first settlement to the present time. A. P. MARVIN. Lancaster, 1879.

Lynn, History of. ALONZO LEWIS and JAMES A. NEWHALL. Boston, 1865.

Malden, The History of. DELORAINCE PENDRE COREY. Malden, 1899.

Middlesex County, Massachusetts, History of. SAMUEL ADAMS DRAKE. Boston, 1880.

Newbury, Massachusetts, History of. JOHN J. CURRIER. Boston, 1902.

Northampton, Massachusetts, History of, from its settlement in 1664. JAMES RUSSELL TRUMBULL. Northampton, 1898.

North Brookfield, Massachusetts, History of. J. H. TEMPLE. North Brookfield, 1887.

Northfield, Massachusetts, History of the town of. J. H. TEMPLE and GEORGE SHELDON. Albany, 1875.

Oxford, Massachusetts, History of the town of. GEORGE F. DANIELS. Oxford, 1892.

Salem, Annals of. JOSEPH B. FELT. Salem, 1845.

Springfield, The First Century of the History of. HENRY M. BURT. Springfield, 1899.

Springfield, History of. MASON A. GREEN. Springfield, 1888.

Sutton, Massachusetts. History of the town of, from 1764 to 1896. WILLIAM A. BENEDICT and HIRAM A. TRACY. Worcester, 1898.
Woburn, History of. SAMUEL SEWALL. Boston, 1868.

Town Records.

Massachusetts. Commissioner of Public Records. Reports on the Custody and Condition of the Public Records of the Parishes, Towns, and Counties, 1885. Boston, 1889.

Amherst, Records of the Town of, 1735-1788. Edited by J. F. JAMESON. Amherst, 1884.

Boston, Record Commissioners, Reports of. Boston, 1881-1905. Town Records and Selectmen's Records, 1634-1700, v. 2 and 7. Town Records, 1701-1813, v. 12, 14, 16, 18, 26, 31, 35. Selectmen's Records, 1701-1798, v. 11, 13, 15, 17, 19, 20, 24, 26.

Braintree, Records of the Town of, 1640-1793. Edited by SAMUEL A. BATES. Randolph, Massachusetts, 1886.

Brookline, Muddy River and Brookline Records, 1634-1838. Boston, 1875.

Cambridge, Massachusetts, The Records of the Town of, 1630-1703. Cambridge, 1901.

Dedham, Massachusetts, The Early Records of the Town of, 1636-1706. Edited by the town clerk, DON GLEASON HILL. Town and Selectmen's Records, v. 3, 4 and 5. Dedham, 1892-1894.

Dorchester, Town Records of, 1631-1687, in Report of the Record Commissioners, Boston, v. 4. Boston, 1880.

Dudley, Massachusetts, Town Records of, 1732-1794. Pawtucket, Rhode Island, 1893. 2 v.

Duxbury, Massachusetts. Copy of the Old Records of the Town of. Plymouth, 1893.

Fitchburg, Massachusetts, The Old Records of the Town of, 1764-1789. Compiled by WALTER A. DAVIS. Fitchburg, 1898. 2 v.

Groton, Massachusetts, The Early Records of, 1662-1707. Edited by SAMUEL A. GREEN. Groton, 1880.

Lancaster, Early Records of, 1643-1725. Edited by HENRY S. NOURSE. Lancaster, 1884.

Lee, The Records of the Town of, 1777-1801. Lee, 1900. (Contains also records of Hopeland School District.)

Lunenberg, Massachusetts, The Early Records of, 1719-1764. Compiled by WALTER A. DAVIS. Fitchburg, 1896.

Manchester, Town Records of, 1636-1786. Salem, 1889. 2 v.

Plymouth, Records of the Town of, 1636-1743. Boston, 1889. 2 v.

Rowley, Early Records of the Town of, 1639-1672. Essex Institute Historical Collections, v. 13, pp. 253-262. Salem, 1876.

Salem, Town Records of. Essex Institute Historical Collections, v. 9, pt. 1., pp. 5-232. Salem, 1868.

Tisbury, Massachusetts, Records of the Town of, 1669-1864. Boston, 1903.

Watertown Records, 1634-1822. Watertown, 1894-1900. 3 v.

Weston, Records of the Town of, 1746-1803. Boston; 1873.

Worcester Town Records, 1722-1848. Edited by FRANKLIN P. RICE. In Worcester Society of Antiquity Collections, 1879-1896 passim.

Unclassified.

American Statistical Association, Collections of. v. 1. Boston, 1847.

SEARS, JOHN HENRY. Geology of Essex County, Massachusetts. Salem, 1905.

SEWALL, SAMUEL, Diary of, in Massachusetts Historical Collections, 5th series. Vols. 5-7.

The Diary and Letters of His Excellency THOMAS HUTCHINSON, Esq., edited by PETER ORLANDO HUTCHINSON. Boston, 1886. 2 v.